# RBT EXAM STUDY GUIDE 2024

*Your Roadmap to Excellence in Registered Behavior Technician Licensure! Expert Q&A, Rigorous Practice Tests, and Bonus Resources.*

## Caden Miller

# Table of Contents

# Introduction

## Brief Overview Of The RBT Certification And Its Significance In The Field Of Behavior Analysis

The field of behavior analysis has seen a significant rise in recognition and demand for skilled professionals who can effectively implement behavioral interventions. Among the certifications available in this domain, the Registered Behavior Technician (RBT) credential stands out as a crucial certification, serving as an entry-level designation for individuals keen on working in the field of applied behavior analysis (ABA).

The RBT certification holds immense significance as it signifies an individual's competency and commitment to the principles and practices of behavior analysis. It's designed for those who play a vital role in the implementation of behavior intervention plans created by Board Certified Behavior Analysts (BCBAs) or Board Certified Assistant Behavior Analysts (BCaBAs). RBTs work directly with clients or students in various settings, aiding in behavior assessment, skill acquisition, and behavior reduction strategies.

The RBT certification acknowledges an individual's proficiency in crucial areas such as ethical considerations, behavior assessment, behavior reduction strategies, and skill acquisition. This certification has become increasingly sought after in educational institutions, clinical settings, community-based organizations, and within home-based services. It not only validates an individual's skills but also opens up numerous career opportunities within the field of behavior analysis.

## Purpose Of The Study Guide

The primary purpose of this study guide is to offer a comprehensive resource for RBT exam preparation. It aims to equip aspiring RBTs with a thorough understanding of the fundamental principles and practical applications of behavior analysis. By delving into various topics, case studies, practice questions, and exam-taking strategies, this guide intends to facilitate a deep comprehension of the core concepts essential for success in the certification exam.

This guide also serves as a reference tool for professionals already working in the field. It provides an opportunity for continuous learning and skill enhancement, ensuring that practitioners remain updated with the latest developments and best practices in behavior analysis.

## Overview of the RBT Exam Structure and Format

The RBT exam is a crucial step towards obtaining certification in behavior analysis. It assesses candidates' understanding and application of ABA principles, ethical considerations, and practical skills necessary for working as competent RBTs. The exam comprises multiple-choice questions, focusing on various domains essential for effective behavior analysis practice.

The content domains covered in the exam typically include:

- Measurement
- Assessment
- Skill Acquisition
- Behavior Reduction
- Documentation and Reporting
- Professional Conduct and Scope of Practice

The RBT exam is structured to evaluate candidates' knowledge across these domains, emphasizing the application of ABA principles in real-world scenarios. It is crucial to understand the exam structure, question formats, and time management strategies to approach the exam confidently and effectively.

In subsequent chapters of this guide, each content domain will be explored in detail, providing comprehensive insights, examples, and practice exercises to aid in thorough preparation for the RBT exam.

The journey toward becoming a Registered Behavior Technician involves dedication, a solid understanding of ABA principles, and the ability to apply these principles effectively. This study guide aims to support individuals in their pursuit of RBT certification by providing a structured and comprehensive approach to mastering the essential concepts and skills required for success in the field of behavior analysis.

# Introduction to Behavior Analysis

## Overview Of Applied Behavior Analysis (ABA)

Applied Behavior Analysis (ABA) is a scientific approach focused on understanding and modifying behavior by applying the principles derived from experimental psychology. It aims to identify functional relationships between behavior and environmental variables to foster positive changes in behavior.

### Components of ABA

1. **Behavioral Assessment:** ABA practitioners conduct comprehensive assessments to identify target behaviors, their antecedents, consequences, and relevant environmental variables. Functional Behavior Assessments (FBAs) are commonly employed to determine the function of behaviors accurately. For instance, in a school setting, a behavioral assessment might involve observing a student's behavior in different contexts to understand triggers and functions of specific behaviors, leading to tailored interventions.

2. **Behavioral Interventions:** Based on assessments, individualized interventions are designed to modify behavior effectively. These interventions often incorporate principles such as reinforcement, shaping, chaining, and prompting to teach new skills and decrease maladaptive behaviors. For instance, in a clinical setting working with a child diagnosed with autism, ABA-based interventions might involve using positive reinforcement (e.g., rewarding desired behaviors with praise or tokens) to encourage social interactions or communication skills.

3. **Data-Driven Decision-Making:** ABA relies heavily on systematic data collection and analysis to assess the efficacy of interventions and make data-informed decisions. Practitioners collect data on behavior frequencies, durations, and antecedents to measure progress and adapt interventions accordingly. For example, in a behavioral therapy program, data might be collected using behavior tracking charts or digital applications to monitor behavior changes over time and refine intervention strategies.

### Applications of ABA

ABA is widely applicable across diverse populations and settings, including but not limited to:

- **Autism Spectrum Disorder (ASD):** ABA is extensively used in treating individuals with ASD, focusing on skill development, behavior reduction, and improving adaptive functioning.
- **Developmental Disabilities:** It is employed in addressing various developmental disorders, intellectual disabilities, and behavioral challenges, aiding individuals in acquiring necessary life skills and reducing problem behaviors.
- **Organizational Behavior Management (OBM):** ABA principles are applied in organizational settings to improve employee performance, enhance workplace culture, and achieve organizational goals by employing behavior modification strategies.

# Fundamental Principles Of Behavior

Understanding behavior necessitates familiarity with fundamental principles:

## Operant Conditioning

One of the fundamental principles in behavior analysis is Operant Conditioning, introduced by B.F. Skinner. It revolves around the relationship between behavior and its outcomes.

- **Positive Reinforcement:** This is providing a pleasurable stimulus after an activity to make that behavior more likely to occur again. For instance, applauding a student for completing their homework on time encourages them to continue the behavior.
- **Negative Reinforcement:** Removal of an aversive stimulus reinforces behavior. For example, a person might take pain medication (behavior) to relieve pain (aversive stimulus), leading to an increase in the behavior of taking medication.
- **Punishment:** Imposing unpleasant consequences to make a behavior less likely to happen again. However, it's essential to note that punishment might suppress behavior temporarily but might not lead to lasting behavioral change.
- **Extinction:** A decline in the incidence of a behavior that was previously encouraged occurs when the conduct is no more accompanied by the repercussion that was previously used to reinforce it. If a youngster is no longer given attention for throwing a tantrum, for instance, the child's behavior of throwing tantrums may finally disappear.

## Classical Conditioning

Ivan Pavlov's classical conditioning theory demonstrates how associations between stimuli can elicit certain responses.

- **Unconditioned Stimulus (UCS) and Unconditioned Response (UCR):** These are natural, unlearned stimuli and responses. For instance, food (UCS) elicits salivation (UCR).
- **Conditioned Stimulus (CS) and Conditioned Response (CR):** A neutral stimulus can be transformed into a conditioned stimulus by repeatedly matching it with an unconditioned stimulus. This transformation results in a conditioned response being elicited. For example, a bell (CS) paired with food (UCS) leads to the bell eliciting salivation (CR) even without food.

## Behavioral Contingencies

Behavioral contingencies emphasize the relationship between behavior and environmental events.

- **Antecedent-Behavior-Consequence (ABC):** This model highlights the three key components in behavior analysis. The behavior is triggered by the predecessor, which is then followed by a repercussion, which will have an effect on the probability that the behavior will occur again. Understanding the ABCs helps in identifying patterns and functional relationships in behavior.

- **Reinforcement Schedules:** A variety of reinforcement schedules, such as fixed ratio and variable interval, influence the rate of behavior as well as the pattern of behavior. A fixed ratio plan, for example, encourages behavior after a predetermined number of responses, whereas a variable ratio schedule reinforces behavior following an undetermined number of responses. Both schedules are examples of behavior reinforcement.

## Applications and Relevance

Understanding these principles is crucial in various settings:

- **Education:** Teachers utilize reinforcement strategies to motivate students and manage classroom behavior effectively.
- **Therapeutic Interventions:** Psychologists and therapists employ these principles to modify behaviors and treat various psychological conditions.
- **Business and Marketing:** Marketers use conditioning principles in advertising and product placement to influence consumer behavior.

## History And Development Of Behavior Analysis

The historical trajectory of behavior analysis is essential for comprehending its evolution:

### Behaviorism's Emergence

The early 20th century marked a significant shift in psychology with the emergence of behaviorism, which aimed to make psychology a more objective science by focusing on observable behavior rather than subjective mental processes.

- **John B. Watson:** Considered the father of behaviorism, Watson advocated for the study of observable behavior and the rejection of introspection. His 1913 paper, "Psychology as the Behaviorist Views It," outlined behaviorism's principles and objectives.

### Contributions of Early Behaviorists

The works of early behaviorists laid the groundwork for behavior analysis and its principles:

- **Ivan Pavlov:** Pavlov's experiments with dogs led to the discovery of classical conditioning, demonstrating how associations between stimuli could lead to conditioned responses. His research significantly influenced the understanding of learning processes.
- **B.F. Skinner:** The work that Skinner did on operational conditioning allowed for a more in-depth comprehension of the ways in which behavior is affected by the repercussions of that activity. He presented the idea of reinforcement and showed how environmental circumstances might have an effect on behavior.

## ABA's Emergence and Development

Applied Behavior Analysis emerged later as a distinct field within behavior analysis:

- **O. Ivar Lovaas:** His pioneering work in the 1960s used behavior analysis principles to develop interventions for children with autism. Lovaas implemented intensive behavioral interventions, including discrete trial training, to teach skills and reduce maladaptive behaviors. His landmark study in 1987 demonstrated the effectiveness of early intensive behavioral intervention (EIBI) for children with autism.
- **The Behavior Analyst Certification Board (BACB):** Formed in 1998, the BACB standardized professional credentials in behavior analysis, including the creation of the Registered Behavior Technician (RBT) credential, establishing ethical guidelines and competency standards.

## Applications and Evolution

Behavior analysis expanded its applications across diverse fields and settings:

- **Education:** Behavior analysis principles are integrated into teaching strategies, shaping classroom management and individualized instruction for students with diverse learning needs.
- **Clinical Settings:** ABA-based interventions are extensively used in clinical settings, especially in autism treatment, focusing on behavior modification, skill acquisition, and enhancing adaptive behaviors.
- **Organizational Behavior Management:** In the workplace, behavior analysis principles are applied to improve employee performance, foster a positive work environment, and enhance organizational outcomes.

# Ethics and Professional Conduct

## Professionalism In Behavior Analysis

Professionalism in behavior analysis encapsulates a spectrum of attributes, behaviors, and ethical considerations that contribute to effective and ethical practice. It encompasses several key facets:

### 1. Commitment to Ethical Guidelines

Behavior analysts and Registered Behavior Technicians (RBTs) adhere to ethical standards set forth by the Behavior Analyst Certification Board (BACB) and professional organizations. This commitment ensures ethical decision-making, confidentiality, and the protection of clients' rights and well-being.

### 2. Competence and Continuing Education

Continuous professional development and the pursuit of competence are fundamental. Behavior analysts and RBTs engage in ongoing learning, seeking opportunities for professional growth through workshops, conferences, courses, and staying updated on the latest research and best practices.

### 3. Accountability and Responsibility

Professionalism involves taking ownership of one's actions and decisions. Behavior analysts and RBTs are accountable for their practice, interventions, data collection, and behavior change procedures. They acknowledge their responsibilities toward clients, ensuring the delivery of effective, evidence-based interventions.

### 4. Effective Communication and Collaboration

Clear, respectful, and empathetic communication forms the bedrock of professionalism. Behavior analysts and RBTs communicate effectively with clients, families, caregivers, multidisciplinary teams, educators, and other professionals involved in the care of the client. Collaborative efforts and transparency in discussions about assessments, interventions, and progress are crucial for successful outcomes.

### 5. Maintaining Professional Boundaries

Establishing and maintaining professional boundaries is vital in behavior analysis practice. Behavior analysts and RBTs ensure that their interactions with clients and their families remain within the scope of professional practice, avoiding dual relationships or conflicts of interest that might compromise the welfare of clients.

### 6. Ethical Decision-Making

Professionalism involves navigating ethical dilemmas with integrity. Behavior analysts and RBTs encounter complex situations where ethical principles might conflict or challenge professional conduct. Making sound decisions that prioritize the well-being of clients while upholding ethical standards is imperative.

**Applications in Practice:**

- **Clinical Settings:** In clinical practice, professionalism ensures that behavior analysts and RBTs deliver interventions that are evidence-based, individualized, and respectful of clients' rights and autonomy.
- **Educational Environments:** Professionalism in behavior analysis within educational settings involves collaboration with educators, effective communication with students and their families, and contributing to Individualized Education Programs (IEPs) while respecting confidentiality and privacy.

**Challenges and Continuous Improvement:**

Maintaining professionalism may present challenges:

- **Work-Life Balance:** Balancing professional responsibilities with personal life requires a conscious effort to avoid burnout and ensure self-care.
- **Ethical Dilemmas:** Behavior analysts and RBTs encounter ethical dilemmas that demand careful consideration and adherence to ethical guidelines.

# Ethical Considerations For RBTs

RBTs operate under the supervision and guidance of Board Certified Behavior Analysts (BCBAs) or Board Certified Assistant Behavior Analysts (BCaBAs). This hierarchical structure ensures that RBTs follow the ethical guidelines established by the Behavior Analyst Certification Board (BACB) and professional organizations. Compliance with these guidelines and maintaining open lines of communication with supervisors ensures ethical standards are met in all aspects of practice.

RBTs receive ongoing guidance in implementing behavior intervention plans (BIPs), conducting assessments, data collection, and intervention strategies. Regular supervision sessions not only ensure adherence to ethical standards but also facilitate professional growth and competence enhancement.

## Informed Consent and Client Autonomy

Obtaining informed consent is a crucial ethical consideration for RBTs. They must ensure that clients or their legal representatives fully understand the nature and purpose of behavior analysis services, the goals of interventions, assessment procedures, potential risks and benefits, and the clients' right to refuse or discontinue services. It is imperative to present information in a clear, understandable manner, respecting the clients' autonomy and decision-making capacity.

Moreover, RBTs continuously involve clients and their families in the decision-making process regarding interventions. They consider and respect the preferences, values, and cultural backgrounds of the clients while developing and implementing behavior change programs.

## Respect for Client Dignity and Rights

RBTs uphold the dignity and rights of their clients throughout their practice. They demonstrate respect and sensitivity in their interactions, recognizing and valuing the individuality of each client. This involves considering the clients' preferences, strengths, and needs when designing interventions, fostering an environment of trust and mutual respect.

Additionally, RBTs ensure that interventions are implemented in a manner that upholds the clients' dignity, avoids reinforcement of stigmatizing behaviors, and promotes the development of socially significant skills that enhance the clients' quality of life.

## Professional Conduct, Competence, and Continuous Learning

Maintaining professionalism is essential for RBTs. Professional conduct involves integrity, reliability, accountability, and honesty in all aspects of practice. RBTs exhibit competence by implementing interventions accurately, adhering to data collection protocols, and using evidence-based practices to address the clients' needs effectively.

Continuous learning and professional development are integral to ensuring ongoing competence and ethical practice. RBTs engage in continuing education, workshops, seminars, and regular updates on research and advancements in behavior analysis. This commitment to learning supports ethical decision-making and ensures that interventions are based on the most current evidence and best practices.

## Confidentiality, Data Handling, and HIPAA Compliance

Preserving client confidentiality and privacy is paramount. RBTs handle sensitive client information with the utmost care, ensuring confidentiality and compliance with the Health Insurance Portability and Accountability Act (HIPAA) regulations. They maintain secure records, use encrypted communication methods, and share client information only with authorized individuals or entities involved in the clients' care.

Proper data collection, storage, and sharing adhere to ethical standards. RBTs ensure accuracy, relevance, and security in handling client data, using it solely for the purpose of treatment and assessment, while respecting clients' privacy rights.

## Ethical Decision-Making and Dilemma Resolution

RBTs encounter various ethical dilemmas that require thoughtful consideration and ethical decision-making. Ethical dilemmas may arise when clients' preferences conflict with recommended interventions or when faced with situations involving ethical boundaries or potential harm to clients.

In such cases, RBTs rely on their ethical decision-making skills, seeking guidance from supervisors or ethical committees, and following a systematic approach to resolve ethical dilemmas. They weigh the potential benefits and risks, always prioritizing the well-being and best interests of the client while upholding ethical standards.

# Maintaining Client Confidentiality And Privacy

In professional practice, safeguarding client confidentiality and privacy is paramount. These ethical principles serve as the foundation of trust between practitioners and clients across diverse fields such as behavior analysis, counseling, psychology, healthcare, and more. Upholding confidentiality ensures the protection of sensitive information shared within the therapeutic or professional relationship.

## Ethical Foundations and Legal Mandates

1. **Ethical Guidelines:** Professional bodies and organizations establish ethical guidelines to govern practitioners' behavior. For instance, the Behavior Analyst Certification Board (BACB) outlines stringent codes of conduct that emphasize maintaining confidentiality as a core ethical principle.

2. **Legal Frameworks:** Laws and regulations, like HIPAA in the United States or similar privacy laws globally, enforce strict confidentiality standards. Professionals are obliged to adhere to these laws, ensuring the protection of client information.

## Elements of Confidentiality and Privacy

1. **Informed Consent:** Before initiating any form of intervention or assessment, practitioners obtain informed consent from clients. This process involves informing clients about the boundaries of confidentiality and circumstances where exceptions might apply, such as instances of imminent harm.

2. **Secure Record-Keeping:** Professionals are responsible for maintaining secure records, including assessment reports, session notes, and personal details. Compliance with privacy laws and ensuring restricted access to authorized personnel is imperative.

3. **Confidential Communication:** Sessions and discussions occur in private settings to maintain confidentiality. Professionals take precautions to prevent unauthorized access or disclosure of sensitive information.

## Ethical Considerations and Best Practices

1. **Professional Boundaries:** Practitioners adhere to clear boundaries concerning client information. Sharing details with third parties without explicit consent is avoided, except in situations where mandated by law or ethical guidelines.

2. **Consent and Collaboration:** Collaborative settings involving multiple professionals require explicit protocols for information sharing while preserving confidentiality. Protocols ensure necessary communication while respecting client privacy.

3. **Digital Confidentiality:** In the digital age, telehealth and electronic communication raise concerns regarding data privacy. Professionals employ encrypted platforms and secure methods to protect electronic communications and data storage.

## Cultural Sensitivity and Confidentiality

Cultural diversity influences individuals' perceptions of confidentiality. Practitioners need cultural competence to understand varying norms and beliefs, respecting these while adhering to ethical standards of confidentiality.

## Challenges and Solutions

1. **Confidentiality in Telehealth:** The advent of telehealth services presents challenges in maintaining confidentiality. Professionals mitigate risks by utilizing secure platforms and effectively communicating data privacy measures to clients.

2. **Interdisciplinary Collaboration:** Collaboration among professionals, while preserving confidentiality, demands clear agreements and protocols. These protocols facilitate necessary communication while ensuring compliance with ethical standards.

## Impact on Client Trust and Treatment Outcomes

Confidentiality breaches significantly impact client trust and treatment outcomes. Upholding confidentiality fosters trust, encourages open communication, and provides a safe environment for clients to address sensitive issues without fear of exposure.

Maintaining client confidentiality and privacy is a cornerstone of ethical practice across professional fields. Upholding these principles promotes trust, ensures client autonomy, and fosters a secure environment for therapeutic or professional relationships.

# Measurement and Data Collection

## Types Of Data Collection Methods

Data collection methods in behavior analysis play a crucial role in understanding, assessing, and modifying behavior. A thorough understanding of various methods is essential for Registered Behavior Technicians (RBTs) to select the most appropriate approach for their specific objectives.

1. **Direct Observation**

This method involves systematically observing and recording behavior as it occurs. It provides real-time data and allows for the analysis of specific behavioral occurrences. RBTs may use different strategies within direct observation, such as continuous recording, partial interval recording, whole interval recording, or momentary time sampling.

- *Continuous Recording*: Involves documenting every instance of behavior within a specified time frame. This method is ideal for behaviors that occur at high frequencies and have a short duration.
- *Interval Recording*: Utilizes time intervals for observation, examples of this include partial interval recording, which records the behavior if it occurs at any time over the interval, and whole interval recording, which records the behavior if it continues within the full interval.

2. **Self-Report and Surveys**

These methods involve gathering information directly from individuals about their behaviors, thoughts, or feelings. While self-reports and surveys can provide valuable insights, they might be subjective and influenced by various factors such as social desirability bias or memory limitations.

- *Interviews*: Structured or semi-structured interviews allow RBTs to gather information through guided conversations with clients or caregivers. Open-ended questions can provide rich qualitative data.
- *Questionnaires and Rating Scales*: Standardized tools with predefined questions or statements allow for quantitative measurement of behaviors or attitudes.

3. **Archival Data Review**

Analyzing existing records or historical data related to the behavior under study. This method can be useful in providing context or baseline information, especially in clinical or educational settings. RBTs may review school records, medical records, or incident reports to gather relevant data.

4. **Technological Tools**

With advancements in technology, RBTs can employ various tools such as wearable devices, mobile applications, or sensors to collect data automatically or semi-automatically. These tools can track behaviors continuously and provide objective measurements, reducing potential biases in data collection.

# Implementing Measurement Procedures

Implementing accurate measurement procedures is critical for RBTs to ensure reliability and validity in collected data. Several key steps are involved in this process:

- **Operational Definitions**: Defining target behaviors in clear, observable, and measurable terms is fundamental. Operational definitions specify what behaviors are to be observed and how they will be recorded.
- **Data Collection Plan**: Developing a comprehensive plan outlining the details of data collection is crucial. This plan includes specifics about the behavior to be measured, the setting, the time frame, the individuals involved, and the data collection method chosen.
- **Interobserver Agreement (IOA)**: Ensuring consistency and reliability in data collection by comparing the results of two or more independent observers. Calculating interobserver agreement percentages helps verify the accuracy of recorded data.
- **Data Collection Training**: Providing thorough training to personnel responsible for data collection is essential. This training includes familiarizing them with the operational definitions, the data collection plan, and specific procedures to ensure accuracy and reliability in their observations and recordings.

# Graphing And Visual Representation Of Data

Graphs serve as indispensable tools in behavior analysis, providing visual representations that elucidate patterns, changes, and trends in behavioral data. Understanding various graphing techniques is pivotal for Registered Behavior Technicians (RBTs) to effectively communicate findings and make data-driven decisions.

## Types of Graphs:

- **Line Graphs**: Widely utilized to portray changes in behavior over time. The x-axis represents time, while the y-axis illustrates frequency, duration, or intensity of the behavior. Line graphs enable RBTs to visualize behavior patterns and alterations across sessions or interventions.
- **Bar Graphs**: Effective for comparing different categories or conditions. RBTs employ bar graphs to showcase behavioral changes across settings, various intervention strategies, or among different individuals.
- **Cumulative Records**: Depict the total count of behaviors over successive observation periods. These records facilitate the identification of overall behavior trends and variations across time.

- **Scatterplots**: Display the relationship between two variables, allowing RBTs to examine correlations between behaviors or environmental factors influencing behavior. Scatterplots help identify potential triggers or associations influencing behavior change.

## Interpreting Graphs:

- **Baseline Behavior Identification**: Graphs provide a clear representation of baseline behavior, offering a reference point to gauge alterations post-intervention. Understanding baseline data aids in assessing the effectiveness of implemented strategies.
- **Trend Detection and Pattern Analysis**: Visualizing data via graphs enables RBTs to detect trends, such as increases, decreases, or stability in behavior over time. Identifying patterns assists in comprehending behavior dynamics and planning targeted interventions.
- **Assessing Intervention Effectiveness**: Comparing pre- and post-intervention data on graphs allows RBTs to evaluate the impact of behavioral modification strategies. This evaluation guides decisions on continuing, modifying, or discontinuing interventions based on their effectiveness.

## Visual Analysis of Data:

- **Utilizing Trend Lines**: Incorporating trend lines on graphs aids RBTs in visually identifying behavioral trends and patterns. These lines facilitate easier interpretation and analysis of data, supporting decision-making processes.
- **Data-Based Decision Making**: RBTs rely on graphed data to make informed decisions. Analyzing graphs assists in determining the success of interventions and enables adjustments to behavior plans for optimal outcomes.
- **Facilitating Communication and Collaboration**: Visual representations of data on graphs foster effective communication among team members, parents, or caregivers. Clear graphical depictions provide a shared understanding of behavior, encouraging collaborative efforts in devising and implementing interventions.

# Assessment and Behavior Reduction

The field of behavior analysis emphasizes the importance of understanding and addressing challenging behaviors in individuals. To improve the quality of life for those who struggle with behavioral issues and to encourage positive behavior change, evaluation, and behavior reduction interventions play an essential role. An overview of the most important ideas pertaining to behavior modification and evaluation is presented in this chapter, including Functional Behavior Assessment (FBA), behavior reduction strategies, and behavior intervention planning.

## Functional Behavior Assessment (FBA)

The FBA is a methodical procedure that is utilized to determine the root cause or reason for a behavior. FBA goes beyond simply describing the form or topography of the behavior; it seeks to understand the environmental variables that influence and maintain the behavior. Developing successful behavior intervention programs is possible for practitioners if they first determine the function of the behavior in question.

FBA typically involves collecting data through direct observation, interviews with relevant individuals, and reviewing existing records. The collected information helps identify patterns, antecedents (triggers), and consequences (reinforcements) associated with the behavior. This analysis provides insight into the function the behavior serves, such as attention-seeking, escape/avoidance, access to tangibles, or automatic reinforcement.

There are several methods and tools used in conducting an FBA. One commonly used method is the ABC analysis, which requires the documentation of the Antecedents, which are the events that occur prior to the behavior, the Behavior itself, and the Consequences, which are the situations that occur right after the behavior. Patterns and possible purposes for the behavior can be identified with the assistance of this study.

Another method used in FBA is the functional analysis, which is an experimental procedure conducted in a controlled setting. During a functional analysis, the antecedents and consequences are manipulated to determine the function of the behavior. This method provides more precise information about the function of the behavior and helps guide the development of effective behavior intervention strategies.

When it comes to establishing appropriate and successful behavior intervention programs, having a solid grasp of the function of the behavior is necessary. There is a possibility that the role of the behavior is not properly determined, the intervention may not effectively address the underlying causes of the behavior and may not lead to lasting behavior change.

## Behavior Reduction Strategies

Once the function of the behavior has been determined through FBA, behavior reduction strategies can be implemented. These strategies aim to decrease or eliminate the problem behavior while teaching alternative, more appropriate behaviors. It is essential to keep in mind that techniques for behavior modification ought to constantly be fabricated on the basis of the specific requirements and qualities of the individual.

Here are some commonly used behavior reduction strategies:

### 1. Positive Behavior Support (PBS)

Positive Behavior Support (PBS) is a method centered on comprehending and dealing with the root reasons behind challenging behaviors. It revolves around establishing a nurturing setting, instructing alternative skills, and employing positive reinforcement to boost desired behaviors while diminishing the occurrence of challenging ones. PBS emphasizes proactive strategies to prevent the occurrence of problem behaviors and promote positive behavior change.

One aspect of PBS is the use of antecedent interventions, which involve modifying the environment to decrease the likelihood of problem behaviors and increase the likelihood of desired behaviors. For example, if a child engages in disruptive behavior during transitions, modifying the environment by providing visual schedules or using transition cues can help reduce the occurrence of the behavior.

Another aspect of PBS is the use of consequence interventions, which involve providing positive reinforcement for desired behaviors and withholding reinforcement for problem behaviors. Reinforcement can be in the form of praise, tokens, access to preferred activities or items, or other reinforcers that are meaningful to the individual.

### 2. Differential Reinforcement

Differential Reinforcement is a technique focused on reinforcing alternative behaviors that are incompatible with the problematic behavior, while refraining from reinforcing the problematic behavior itself. The objective is to educate and reinforce more suitable behaviors that fulfill the same purpose as the problematic one.

For instance, if a child exhibits aggressive behavior to garner attention, the practitioner can educate and reinforce proper methods of seeking attention, like raising their hand or politely asking for help. Through reinforcing these appropriate behaviors and disregarding or offering minimal attention to the problematic behavior, the child learns more adaptive ways of accomplishing their objectives.

### 3. Extinction

Extinction involves withholding reinforcement for a problem behavior, leading to a decrease in its occurrence. This strategy is effective when the problem behavior is maintained by attention, escape/avoidance, or access to tangibles, and the reinforcer can be reasonably withheld.

When implementing extinction, it is important to be consistent and ensure that the reinforcer for the problem behavior is consistently withheld. Initially, there may be an increase in the problem behavior, known as an extinction burst, as the individual tests whether the behavior will still produce the desired outcome. However, with continued consistency, the behavior should decrease over time.

It is important to note that extinction should only be used when the reinforcer is not necessary or when alternative, more adaptive behaviors can be taught and reinforced. In some cases, extinction may not be appropriate or effective, and alternative strategies should be considered.

### 4. Response Cost

Response Cost involves removing a specific reinforcer following the occurrence of a problem behavior. The individual experiences a cost or loss as a consequence of engaging in the problem behavior. This strategy aims to decrease the occurrence of the behavior by associating it with the loss of a preferred privilege or token.

For example, in a token economy system, if a student engages in off-task behavior during class, they may lose a token that can be exchanged for a preferred activity or item. By removing the token as a consequence of the problem behavior, the student learns that engaging in the behavior results in the loss of the opportunity to access preferred items or activities.

Response cost can bean effective strategy for behaviors that are maintained by access to preferred items or activities. It provides a clear consequence for the problem behavior and teaches the individual that engaging in the behavior leads to a loss of privileges.

### 5. Functional Communication Training (FCT)

Functional Communication Training (FCT) concentrates on instructing individuals on alternative and more suitable methods to express their needs or wants. This approach proves highly effective for individuals who exhibit challenging behaviors to obtain attention or desired items.

FCT entails educating the individual on a communication response that fulfills the same purpose as the challenging behavior. For example, if a child throws tantrums to acquire a favored toy, the practitioner can teach the child to verbally request the toy or use a communication device. By imparting alternative communication skills, the motivation behind engaging in the challenging behavior diminishes.

## Behavior Intervention Planning

Behavior intervention planning involves developing a comprehensive plan to address the target behavior based on the information gathered through FBA. A well-designed behavior intervention plan incorporates the following steps:

### 1. Setting Goals

Clear and measurable goals are established for behavior reduction. These goals should be specific, observable, and relevant to the individual's needs. Setting realistic goals helps guide the behavior intervention process and provides a framework for evaluating progress.

### 2. Selecting Strategies

Based on the function of the behavior and the identified antecedents and consequences, appropriate behavior reduction strategies are selected. These strategies may include a combination of positive reinforcement, teaching alternative skills, modifying the environment, and implementing consequences. The selection of strategies should align with the individual's unique needs and characteristics.

It is important to consider the individual's strengths, preferences, and cultural background when selecting strategies. Strategies should be evidence-based and grounded in the principles of behavior analysis.

### 3. Implementation

The behavior intervention plan is implemented consistently across all relevant settings and by all individuals involved in the individual's life. Collaboration and communication between caregivers, teachers, and other professionals are crucial for successful implementation. Consistency in the application of strategies enhances the effectiveness of the behavior intervention plan.

Training and support may be provided to individuals implementing the behavior intervention plan to ensure fidelity and effectiveness. Ongoing monitoring and supervision can help address any challenges or modifications that may be needed during implementation.

## 4. Monitoring and Evaluation

The effectiveness of the behavior intervention plan is continuously monitored and evaluated. Data are collected to assess the progress towards the goals and to make any necessary adjustments to the strategies. Monitoring allows practitioners to track the individual's response to the intervention and make data-driven decisions.

Data collection methods may include direct observation, behavior rating scales, and interviews with relevant individuals. The frequency and duration of data collection depend on the individual's needs and the complexity of the behavior. Regular team meetings may be held to review progress, discuss challenges, and make adjustments to the intervention plan.

## 5. Generalization and Maintenance

Once the problem behavior is effectively reduced, efforts are made to generalize the new skills and behaviors to different settings and individuals. Generalization involves ensuring that the individual can demonstrate the desired behaviors in various contexts, with different people, and across different tasks or activities.

Generalization strategies may include providing opportunities for practice in various settings, fading prompts and supports, and teaching self-monitoring and self-management skills. It is important to systematically plan for generalization from the beginning of the intervention and continue to monitor and support generalization throughout the process.

Maintenance strategies are implemented to ensure that the behavior change is sustained over time, promoting long-term positive outcomes. These strategies may include periodic check-ins, booster sessions, and ongoing support and reinforcement. Monitoring and evaluating the maintenance of behavior change is critical to prevent regression and promote continued progress.

# Skill Acquisition and Behavior Change

In the field of behavior analysis, skill acquisition refers to the process of teaching individuals new skills to replace problem behaviors or to enhance their repertoire of adaptive behaviors. Skill acquisition programs are designed to teach a wide range of skills, comprising academic, communication, social, self-help, and vocational skills. These programs depend on the principles of behavior analysis, which emphasize systematic instruction, reinforcement, and the use of evidence-based strategies.

Skill acquisition programs are particularly beneficial for individuals with developmental disabilities, such as autism spectrum disorder, who may require explicit and structured instruction to acquire new skills. The goal of these programs is to enhance the individual's independence, functional abilities, and overall quality of life.

In this chapter, we will explore strategies for teaching new skills, behavior change procedures, and prompting and fading techniques commonly used in skill acquisition programs. These strategies and techniques have been proven effective in promoting skill development and behavior change.

## Strategies for Teaching New Skills

Effective teaching strategies play a vital role in skill acquisition programs. The following strategies are commonly used to teach new skills:

### 1. Task Analysis

Task analysis is the process of deconstructing a complicated skill into smaller, more achievable steps. This method enables instructors to teach each step in a structured manner, offering instant feedback and reinforcement. It proves especially beneficial for instructing skills with numerous sequential stages, like brushing teeth, tying shoelaces, or solving math problems.

Breaking down the skill into manageable steps allows individuals to grasp and excel at each step before progressing to the next. Additionally, task analysis aids in pinpointing any particular challenges or sections that might need extra assistance or guidance.

For example, when teaching a child to tie shoelaces, the task analysis may include the following steps: (1) cross the laces, (2) make loops with each lace, (3) cross the loops, (4) tuck one loop under the other, and (5) tighten the knot. By teaching each step individually and providing practice and reinforcement, the child can gradually acquire the skill of tying shoelaces.

### 2. Chaining

Chaining is a strategy that involves teaching a skill by linking individual steps together to form a complete sequence. There are two main types of chaining: forward chaining and backward chaining.

Forward chaining involves teaching the first step of the skill sequence and gradually adding subsequent steps. For example, when teaching a child to get dressed, the first step may be putting on socks. Once the child masters this step, the instructor adds the next step, such as putting on pants, and continues until the entire dressing routine is mastered.

Backward chaining, on the other hand, involves teaching the last step of the skill sequence first and gradually adding preceding steps. For example, in teaching a child to make a sandwich, the instructor initially demonstrates the final step of assembling the sandwich. Then, the instructor adds the step before the final one, such as spreading the condiments, and continues until the entire sandwich-making process is mastered.

Chaining allows individuals to learn and practice each step of the skill while gradually building toward the complete skill sequence. It provides a clear structure and helps individuals understand the relationship between different steps in a task.

### 3. Errorless Teaching

Errorless teaching is a method that is designed to eliminate the possibility of mistakes occurring throughout the learning process. The process entails supplying the individual with prompts or indications in order to direct their responses, ensuring correct responses are reinforced and errors are minimized.

In errorless teaching, prompts are initially provided at a high level of support to ensure a correct response. As the individual becomes more proficient, prompts are gradually faded, reducing the level of support. Errorless teaching is particularly effective for individuals who may be prone to errors or have difficulty with independent responding.

For example, when teaching a child to identify different colors, the instructor may initially provide a physical prompt by pointing to the correct color while saying its name (e.g., "This is red"). Once the child consistently responds correctly with the physical prompt, the instructor can fade the prompt by pointing without touching the color. Eventually, the child will be able to identify colors independently.

### 4. Discrete Trial Training (DTT)

Discrete Trial Training is a highly structured teaching method that involves breaking down skills into discrete components and using repetition, prompting, and reinforcement to teach each component. DTT is often used to teach skills such as receptive and expressive language, imitation, and academic tasks.

During a discrete trial, the instructor presents a clear instruction or cue (known as the discriminative stimulus), prompts the individual's response if needed, provides immediate feedback, and delivers reinforcement for correct responses. Each trial is presented in a consistent and controlled manner, allowing for repeated practice and reinforcement.

DTT is characterized by its structured format, emphasis on repetition, and systematic use of prompts and reinforcement. It is particularly effective for individuals who benefit from explicit instruction and frequent opportunities for practice.

## Behavior Change Procedures

In addition to teaching new skills, behavior change procedures are used to decrease problem behaviors and promote more adaptive behaviors. The following behavior change procedures are commonly employed in skill acquisition programs:

### 1. Reinforcement

Reinforcement is a fundamental component of behavior change procedures. It works by giving outcomes that boost the chances of a behavior happening again later. There are two types: positive and negative.

Positive reinforcement means giving a reward or something good after a behavior. For instance, a child getting praise or a treat for finishing a task or showing a wanted behavior. This kind of reinforcement strengthens the link between the behavior and the positive result, making the behavior more likely to happen again.

Negative reinforcement involves removing or avoiding something unpleasant after a behavior. For example, a child being allowed to skip a hard task or a loud noise stopping when they do a specific behavior. This type of reinforcement increases the likelihood of the behavior happening again by taking away or avoiding an unpleasant thing.

Reinforcement is a great tool for changing behavior and learning new skills. It helps people understand the effects of what they do and encourages them to repeat positive behaviors.

## 2. Extinction

Extinction is a method of behavior modification that includes deferring reinforcement for a behavior that was formerly reinforced. If a behavior that was previously reinforced does not generate the expected repercussions, then the behavior is no longer, it gradually decreases in frequency and eventually ceases.

Extinction might be difficult because individuals may first demonstrate an increase in the behavior (also known as an extinction burst) as they strive to achieve the formerly reinforced consequence. This can make the process of destruction more difficult. If, on the other hand, the behavior does not regularly result in reinforcement, then it will ultimately become less noticeable.

Extinction is commonly used to decrease problem behaviors that are maintained by attention or other forms of reinforcement. By withholding reinforcement for problem behaviors and redirecting attention to fitting alternative behaviors, individuals learn that participating in the problem behavior no longer produces the desired outcome.

## 3. Differential Reinforcement

The process of reinforcing certain behaviors whilst reserving reinforcement for other behaviors is referred to as using differential reinforcement. This procedure aims to increase the frequency of desirable behaviors while decreasing the occurrence of problem behaviors.

Among the several techniques that fall under the category of differential reinforcement, there are three distinct types: differential reinforcement of alternative behavior (DRA), differential reinforcement of incompatible behavior (DRI), and differential reinforcement of other behavior (DRO).

DRA involves reinforcing an alternative behavior that serves the same function as the problem behavior. For example, if a child engages in disruptive behaviors to gain attention, the instructor may reinforce appropriate requests for attention instead.

DRI involves reinforcing a behavior that is incompatible with the problem behavior. For instance, if a child engages in hand flapping, which interferes with social interaction, the instructor may reinforce engaging in appropriate play behavior that requires both hands.

DRO involves reinforcing the absence of the problem behavior during specific time intervals. For example, if a child engages in self-injurious behaviors, the instructor may reinforce the child for not engaging in the behavior for a certain period of time.

Differential reinforcement procedures effectively target problem behaviors while promoting the development of more adaptive and socially appropriate behaviors.

# Prompting and Fading Techniques

Prompting and fading techniques are used to provide guidance and support during the initial stages of skill acquisition while gradually reducing the level of assistance. These techniques help individuals acquire new skills and promote independence. The following are commonly used prompting and fading techniques:

### 1. Physical Prompts

Physical prompts involve physically guiding the individual's movements to perform a specific behavior. Physical prompts may include hand-over-hand assistance or gently manipulating the individual's body to complete a task. Physical prompts are typically used when an individual has limited motor skills or understanding of the desired behavior.

As the individual becomes more proficient, physical prompts are gradually faded by reducing the amount of physical guidance provided. This allows the individual to gain independence and perform the behavior with minimal or no physical assistance.

### 2. Verbal Prompts

Verbal prompts involve providing verbal cues or instructions to guide the individual's behavior. Verbal prompts may include giving explicit instructions, asking questions, or providing hints or cues. Verbal prompts are useful for individuals who have a better understanding of language and can follow spoken instructions.

Similar to physical prompts, verbal prompts are faded gradually by reducing the level of verbal guidance. The individual is encouraged to respond more independently and rely less on verbal cues over time.

### 3. Visual Prompts

Visual prompts involve using visual aids or cues to support the individual's behavior. Visual prompts can be in the form of written instructions, pictures, symbols, or visual schedules. Visual prompts are particularly helpful for individuals who have better visual processing skills or who benefit from visual supports.

Visual prompts can be gradually faded by reducing the size or clarity of the visual cues or by removing them altogether. The goal is for the individual to perform the behavior without relying on visual prompts.

### 4. Gestural Prompts

Gestural prompts involve using hand or body gestures to guide the individual's behavior. Gestural prompts may include pointing, nodding, or gesturing in the direction of the desired response. Gestural prompts are effective for individuals who have good visual attention and can interpret and respond to gestures.

Similar to other prompting techniques, gestural prompts are faded gradually by reducing the frequency or clarity of the gestures. The individual is encouraged to respond without relying on gestural cues.

# Documentation and Reporting

Effective documentation and reporting play a vital role in behavior analysis. Accurate and comprehensive records provide valuable information about the progress and outcomes of behavior intervention programs. They facilitate communication among team members, allow for data-driven decision-making, and ensure accountability. In this chapter, we will explore the importance of record-keeping in behavior analysis, discuss the process of writing behavioral reports and progress notes, and highlight the significance of effective communication with supervisors and team members.

## Record-Keeping in Behavior Analysis

Record-keeping is an essential aspect of behavior analysis as it enables the collection, analysis, and interpretation of data related to behavior interventions. Clear and thorough documentation serves several purposes, facilitating effective behavior analysis practices across various settings.

### Data Collection and Analysis

Accurate and consistent data collection is crucial for behavior analysis. It allows behavior analysts to track progress, evaluate intervention effectiveness, and make informed decisions about treatment strategies. Records provide a historical record of behavior and intervention data, which helps identify patterns and trends over time.

Behavior analysts utilize various data collection methods, such as direct observation, checklists, rating scales, and electronic data recording systems. These methods help track behaviors, measure target skills, and monitor progress towards goals. Every data collection method possesses its own set of advantages and drawbacks. Behavior analysts must select the most suitable method by considering the unique requirements of the individual and the intervention's context.

Furthermore, data analysis is an integral part of record-keeping. Behavior analysts use statistical and graphical techniques to analyze the collected data, identify trends, and measure the effectiveness of interventions. By systematically analyzing data, behavior analysts can determine whether interventions are producing the desired outcomes and make data-driven decisions to modify or adjust their approaches when necessary.

### Treatment Integrity and Accountability

Documentation ensures treatment integrity by documenting the fidelity of intervention implementation. Behavior analysts record detailed information about the delivery of interventions, including the procedures used, the frequency and duration of sessions, and any modifications made. This documentation allows for ongoing monitoring of treatment fidelity and helps maintain accountability.

Tracking treatment integrity is crucial because it ensures that interventions are implemented as intended and that any deviations from the protocol are documented and addressed. By monitoring treatment integrity, behavior analysts can identify potential issues or discrepancies that may affect intervention outcomes. It also helps in training and supervising staff members involved in the implementation of behavior intervention programs, ensuring consistency and adherence to established protocols.

Additionally, documentation plays a vital role in maintaining accountability, both ethically and legally. Accurate and comprehensive records provide evidence of the delivery of services, informed consent, and adherence to ethical standards. They also facilitate compliance with regulations such as HIPAA (Health Insurance Portability and Accountability Act) and FERPA (Family Educational Rights and Privacy Act), ensuring that individuals' privacy and rights are protected.

## Writing Behavioral Reports and Progress Notes

Behavioral reports and progress notes are important components of documentation in behavior analysis. They provide a summary of the individual's progress, intervention strategies, and outcomes. Well-written reports and notes enable effective communication among team members, support data-driven decision-making, and contribute to the overall success of behavior analysis interventions.

- **Clear and Objective Language**

Behavioral reports and progress notes should use clear and concise language to describe behaviors, interventions, and outcomes. It is important to use objective language that is free from personal biases or interpretations. Descriptions should be based on observable and measurable behavior.

Using objective language ensures that the information documented accurately represents the individual's behaviors and progress. Avoiding subjective interpretations or assumptions helps maintain the integrity and credibility of the reports and notes. Behavior analysts should focus on describing observable behaviors, environmental context, and measurable outcomes to provide a comprehensive understanding of the individual's progress.

- **Structure and Organization**

Reports and progress notes should follow a structured and organized format. This facilitates understanding and allows for easy reference. Common sections in behavioral reports may include client information, background history, assessment results, intervention goals, intervention strategies, progress monitoring data, and recommendations for future interventions.

By following a consistent structure and organization, behavior analysts ensure that the information is presented in a logical and coherent manner. This helps readers, including supervisors and team members, quickly locate and understand the information they need. Additionally, a well-organized structure supports the effective analysis and interpretation of the data presented in the reports and notes.

- **Data Presentation and Analysis**

Behavioral reports and progress notes should present data in a clear and meaningful manner. Graphs, charts, and tables can be utilized to visually represent data and trends over time. Data analysis should include a discussion of progress towards goals, any notable changes in behavior, and the effectiveness of intervention strategies.

Visual representations of data help to highlight patterns, trends, and changes in behavior over time. Graphs and charts provide a visual summary that is easier to interpret and understand compared to raw data alone. Additionally, behavior analysts should provide a detailed analysis of the data, including an interpretation of progress, any challenges encountered, and the effectiveness of intervention strategies implemented. This analysis allows for informed decision-making and the identification of areas that may require adjustments or modifications in the intervention plan.

- **Objective Observations**

Observations and descriptions of behavior should be objective and based on direct observation. Avoid making assumptions or interpretations about the individual's thoughts, feelings, or motivations. Stickto observable behaviors and their environmental context.

Objective observations in behavioral reports and progress notes ensure accuracy and reliability. Behavior analysts should focus on describing what they directly observe, such as specific behaviors, their frequency, duration, and intensity. It is essential to avoid subjective interpretations or assumptions about the individual's internal states or motivations, as these cannot be directly observed. By maintaining objectivity in observations, behavior analysts provide a factual account of the individual's behavior, supporting the validity and credibility of the documentation.

- **Collaboration and Team Communication**

Behavioral reports and progress notes serve as a means of communication among team members involved in the intervention process. Effective communication fosters collaboration, coordination, and shared decision-making. It is essential to ensure that reports and notes are shared with relevant team members in a timely manner.

Collaboration among team members is crucial for the success of behavior analysis interventions. By sharing behavioral reports and progress notes, team members stay informed about the individual's progress, intervention strategies, and outcomes. This shared knowledge allows for a coordinated approach, where team members can provide support, offer insights, and make informed decisions based on the documented information. Timely communication ensures that team members are up to date with the latest developments, enabling them to provide appropriate and consistent support to the individual.

## Communication with Supervisors and Team Members

Effective communication with supervisors and team members is crucial for the success of behavior analysis interventions. Open and transparent communication fosters collaboration, ensures consistency in intervention implementation, and supports the overall effectiveness of the behavior analysis team.

### 1. Regular Team Meetings

Regular team meetings provide an opportunity for team members, including behavior analysts, supervisors, caregivers, and other professionals, to discuss progress, share information, and address concerns. These meetings foster collaboration, ensure consistency in intervention implementation, and allow for the exchange of ideas and feedback.

Team meetings serve as a platform for team members to come together, share their observations and insights, and discuss the individual's progress. These meetings provide a space for brainstorming ideas, troubleshooting challenges, and collectively problem-solving. Regular team meetings promote a sense of unity, shared responsibility, and a collaborative approach to behavior analysis interventions.

## 2. Clear and Timely Communication

Clear and timely communication is essential to keep team members informed about the individual's progress, changes in behavior plans, and updates in intervention strategies. Utilize various communication methods such as in-person meetings, phone calls, emails, and secure messaging platforms to ensure effective information exchange.

Behavior analysts should establish clear channels of communication with supervisors and team members. They should proactively share updates, progress reports, and changes in intervention plans in a timely manner. Clear and concise communication minimizes misunderstandings, ensures that everyone is on the same page, and allows for prompt adjustments or modifications to interventions if necessary. Timely communication also demonstrates professionalism, reliability, and a commitment to collaborative teamwork.

## 3. Documentation Sharing

Sharing relevant documentation, such as behavioral reports, progress notes, and data graphs, with supervisors and team members promotes transparency and allows for informed decision-making. Accessible and up-to-date documentation ensures that everyone involved in the intervention is aware of the individual's progress and can provide appropriate support.

Behavior analysts should make it a priority to share relevant documentation with supervisors and team members. This includes providing copies of behavioral reports, progress notes, and any other relevant documentation that can contribute to the team's understanding of the individual's progress and intervention strategies. Sharing documentation fosters transparency, encourages feedback and input from team members, and supports collaborative decision-making.

## 4. Feedback and Support

Providing constructive feedback and support to team members is crucial for maintaining a positive and collaborative work environment. Behavior analysts should offer guidance, encouragement, and resources to team members, fostering professional growth and ensuring the effective implementation of behavior interventions.

Behavior analysts play a vital role in providing support and mentorship to team members involved in behavior analysis interventions. They should provide constructive feedback on performance, help address challenges, and offer guidance on implementing interventions effectively. By creating a supportive and empowering environment, behavior analysts contribute to the professional growth of team members and ensure the consistent delivery of high-quality behavior analysis services.

## 5. Professional Development Opportunities

Behavior analysts should actively seek professional development opportunities to enhance their communication skills. Training programs, workshops, and conferences can provide valuable insights and techniques for effective communication with supervisors and team members. Continued learning and growth in this area contribute to the overall success of behavior analysis interventions.

Continual professional development is essential for behavior analysts to stay up to date with the latest research, approaches, and techniques in behavior analysis. Attending training programs, workshops, and conferences focused on communication skills equips behavior analysts with the necessary tools and strategies to enhance their interactions with supervisors and team members. Professional development opportunities also provide networking opportunities, allowing behavior analysts to connect with peers and learn from their experiences.

# Supervision and Collaboration

Supervision and collaboration are critical aspects of providing high-quality services in the field of behavior analysis. This chapter delves into the roles and responsibilities of Registered Behavior Technicians (RBTs), emphasizes the importance of collaboration within a multidisciplinary team, explores the process of receiving and implementing feedback, and highlights the ethical considerations involved. Effective supervision and collaboration contribute to the professional growth of RBTs, ensure consistent implementation of behavior interventions, and promote positive outcomes for individuals receiving behavior analysis services.

## Roles and Responsibilities of RBTs

As integral members of the behavior analysis team, Registered Behavior Technicians (RBTs) play a crucial role in the implementation of behavior analysis interventions. They work under the supervision of Board Certified Behavior Analysts (BCBAs) and contribute to the assessment, measurement, and intervention processes. The following are key roles and responsibilities of RBTs:

### 1. Implementing Behavior Intervention Plans (BIPs)

One of the primary responsibilities of RBTs is to carry out behavior intervention plans developed by BCBAs. They diligently follow the strategies and procedures outlined in the BIPs to address the target behaviors and teach new skills. This includes implementing behavior reduction procedures, teaching replacement behaviors, collecting data on target behaviors, and maintaining accurate records.

RBTs must demonstrate proficiency in implementing the specific procedures outlined in the BIPs. They should follow ethical guidelines, maintain client confidentiality, and ensure the safety and well-being of the individuals they serve. RBTs collaborate closely with BCBAs for the purpose of ensuring that the interventions are carried out in a faithful manner and making any changes that are required according to the feedback and interpretation of the data.

### 2. Collecting Data and Monitoring Progress

Accurate data collection is a crucial responsibility of RBTs. They collect data on target behaviors and skill acquisition, following the data collection procedures established by BCBAs. RBTs should be proficient in using data collection tools, such as event recording, duration recording, and interval recording, to measure behavior and track progress over time.

RBTs also play a pivotal role in monitoring progress towards individual goals. They contribute to the ongoing assessment of behavior change by collecting data, graphing and analyzing the data, and reporting the findings to the supervising BCBA. This collaboration ensures that interventions are effective, progress is tracked, and adjustments can be made when necessary.

### 3. Implementing Behavior Management Strategies

RBTs are responsible for implementing behavior management strategies to maintain a safe and structured environment. This includes setting up the physical environment, establishing routines, implementing reinforcement systems, and managing challenging behaviors.

RBTs should be knowledgeable about behavior management techniques and strategies. They should be proficient in implementing positive reinforcement, prompting and fading procedures, and behavior-specific praise. RBTs work closely with BCBAs to understand the individual's behavior support needs and implement appropriate strategies to address challenging behaviors effectively.

### 4. Collaborating with Families and Caregivers

RBTs play a vital role in collaborating with families and caregivers. They provide support and guidance to families in implementing behavior strategies in the home and community settings. RBTs communicate with families regularly, ensuring that they are informed about the individual's progress, goals, and intervention strategies.

Collaboration with families and caregivers promotes consistency and generalization of skills across different environments. RBTs should establish effective lines of communication, provide resources and training to families, and address any concerns or questions they may have. By working collaboratively with families, RBTs can enhance the overall effectiveness of behavior analysis interventions.

## Collaboration Within a Multidisciplinary Team

Behavior analysis interventions often involve collaboration with professionals from various disciplines. Multidisciplinary collaboration ensures a comprehensive and holistic approach to addressing individuals' needs. Here are some key aspects of collaboration within a multidisciplinary team:

### 5. Clear Communication and Shared Goals

Effective collaboration demands clear communication, especially when working with professionals from various disciplines. It's crucial for every team member to grasp their roles, duties, and the common objectives of the intervention. This involves consistent team meetings, email exchanges, and sharing documentation to guarantee everyone is aligned.

Successful collaboration relies on communication strategies like active listening, respecting diverse viewpoints, and articulating information clearly and succinctly. These strategies foster an environment where everyone comprehends and contributes effectively.

### 6. Role Clarity and Task Allocation

Within a multidisciplinary team, it is crucial to establish role clarity and allocate tasks effectively. Each team member should have a defined role and responsibilities based on their area of expertise. This ensures that the intervention plan is implemented consistently and that each team member can contribute their unique skills and knowledge to the process.

Collaboration involves recognizing and respecting the expertise of each team member. RBTs should understand their scope of practice and defer to professionals from other disciplines when necessary. By working collaboratively and recognizing the strengths of each team member, the intervention team can provide comprehensive and effective support to individuals receiving behavior analysis services.

### 7. Regular Team Meetings and Case Consultation

Regular team meetings and case consultations are valuable opportunities for collaboration and information sharing. The members of the team are able to talk about the progress that has been made, present any updates that have been made, and address any issues or concerns that are associated with the intervention at these gatherings.

During team meetings, RBTs can report on the implementation of behavior intervention plans, share data, and seek guidance from other team members. BCBAs can provide feedback, make adjustments to the intervention plan if needed, and ensure that all team members are aligned with the goals and strategies.

### 8. Integration of Treatment Approaches

Behavior analysis interventions often intersect with other therapeutic approaches or disciplines. Collaborating with professionals from other disciplines, such as speech therapists, occupational therapists, or psychologists, allows for a comprehensive and integrated treatment approach.

By integrating different treatment approaches, the team can address a wider range of needs and promote generalization of skills across various settings. Collaborating with professionals from other disciplines involves sharing information, coordinating efforts, and aligning strategies to ensure a cohesive and effective intervention plan.

## Receiving and Implementing Feedback

Receiving and implementing feedback is a crucial aspect of professional growth for RBTs. Feedback provides valuable insights and opportunities for improvement. Here are some key considerations when receiving and implementing feedback:

1. **Openness and Receptiveness:** RBTs should approach feedback with an open mind and receptiveness. They should recognize that feedback is not a personal attack but rather an opportunity for growth and improvement. Being open to feedback demonstrates a commitment to professional development and a willingness to enhance skills and competencies.

2. **Active Listening and Reflection:** When receiving feedback, active listening is essential. RBTs should fully engage in the conversation, ask clarifying questions, and seek to understand the perspective of the person providing feedback. Reflecting on the feedback received helps RBTs gain insights into their performance, identify areas for improvement, and develop action plans to address any concerns or suggestions.

3. **Openness to Feedback**: RBTs should welcome feedback with an open mind, acknowledging that it isn't a personal criticism but an opportunity for growth. Embracing feedback showcases a dedication to professional advancement and a readiness to enhance skills and proficiencies.

4. **Active Listening and Reflection:** During feedback sessions, active listening is paramount for RBTs. Engaging fully in conversations, asking for clarification, and understanding the feedback provider's viewpoint are crucial. Reflecting on feedback helps RBTs comprehend their performance, pinpoint areas for enhancement, and formulate action plans to address concerns or suggestions.

5. **Action Planning and Implementation**: After receiving feedback, RBTs should develop action plans to implement the recommended changes or improvements. This may involve collaborating with the supervising BCBA to identify specific strategies or seeking additional training or resources to enhance skills in certain areas.

Implementing feedback requires a proactive approach and a commitment to continuous learning. RBTs should take ownership of their professional development and actively seek opportunities to refine their skills and knowledge.

### Ethical Considerations

Supervision and collaboration in behavior analysis come with ethical considerations that must be upheld to ensure the welfare and rights of individuals receiving services. Here are some ethical considerations relevant to supervision and collaboration:

1. **Confidentiality and Privacy:** RBTs must uphold client confidentiality and privacy at all times. They should maintain the confidentiality of client information and only share necessary information with team members involved in the intervention. RBTs should follow the guidelines set forth by relevant laws and ethical codes, such as the Health Insurance Portability and Accountability Act (HIPAA).

2. **Competence and Scope of Practice:** RBTs should recognize and work within their scope of practice. They should only implement interventions and strategies that they are competent in and have received appropriate training and supervision for. If a situation arises that falls outside their scope of practice, they should consult with the supervising BCBA or refer the matter to a qualified professional.

3. **Collaboration and Respect for Diversity:** Collaboration within a multidisciplinary team necessitates respect for diversity and cultural sensitivity. RBTs should be aware of and respect the cultural, ethnic, and individual differences of the individuals they serve and their families. They should collaborate with professionals from diverse backgrounds and demonstrate respect for differing perspectives and approaches.

4. **Professional Boundaries:** Maintaining professional boundaries is essential for RBTs. They should establish clear boundaries with clients, families, and other professionals to ensure appropriate relationships and ethical conduct. RBTs should avoid dual relationships and conflicts of interest that could compromise their objectivity, professional judgment, or the welfare of the individuals they serve.

# Exam Preparation Strategies

This chapter focuses on exam preparation strategies specifically designed for the RBT exam. It explores effective test-taking strategies and provides tips for managing exam anxiety. By implementing these strategies, aspiring RBTs can increase their chances of success and perform at their best on the exam.

## Test-Taking Strategies

Test-taking strategies are techniques and approaches that students can employ during the actual exam to improve their performance and maximize their scores. Here are some effective test-taking strategies:

### 1. Understand the Exam Format

Familiarize yourself with the format and structure of the RBT exam. Understand the number of questions, time limit, and question types (e.g., multiple-choice, scenario-based). This knowledge will help you prepare and allocate your time effectively during the exam.

### 2. Review the RBT Task List

The RBT Task List outlines the knowledge and skills required for the RBT exam. Thoroughly review each task area and identify your strengths and weaknesses. Focus on areas where you need more practice and allocate more study time to those topics.

### 3. Utilize Study Materials

Make use of dependable study materials like the RBT Competency Assessment or approved study guides when getting ready for the exam. These resources offer a thorough review of the exam content and assist in organizing your study schedule efficiently.

### 4. Create a Study Schedule

Develop a study schedule that allows you to cover all the content areas systematically. Break down the RBT Task List into smaller study sessions and allocate specific time slots for each topic. This approach ensures that you cover all the necessary material and avoid last-minute cramming.

### 5. Practice with Sample Questions

Practice with sample questions that reflect the format and difficulty level of the RBT exam. This will familiarize you with the types of questions you may encounter and help you develop effective strategies for answering them. Consider using online resources, study guides, or practice exams to access sample questions.

### 6. Seek Clarification

If you come across challenging concepts or tasks during your study, seek clarification from reliable sources. Consult textbooks, online resources, or reach out to experienced professionals or instructors for clarification. Understanding difficult topics thoroughly will boost your confidence and improve your performance on the exam.

## 7. Review and Reflect

Regularly review the material you have covered throughout your study period. Practice active recall by summarizing key concepts, teaching the material to someone else, or creating flashcards. Regular review and reflection help reinforce your understanding and retention of the information.

# Tips for Managing Exam Anxiety

Exam anxiety is a common experience for many students and can negatively impact performance. Here are some tips to help manage exam anxiety:

## 1. Be Prepared

Thorough preparation is the key to managing exam anxiety. Follow your study schedule, cover all the necessary material, and engage in regular practice. Knowing that you have thoroughly prepared will boost your confidence and reduce anxiety.

## 2. Time Management

Plan your time effectively during the exam. Read through all the questions quickly at the beginning and allocate time for each question based on its complexity and point value. Managing your time well will prevent rushing through questions and reduce anxiety.

## 3. Relaxation Techniques

Practice relaxation methods before and during the exam to ease your mind and reduce anxiety. Try deep breathing exercises, progressive muscle relaxation, or mindfulness meditation. Integrate these into your study routine for familiarity.

## 4. Positive Self-Talk

Challenge negative thoughts with positive affirmations. Remind yourself of your preparations, knowledge, and skills. Have faith in your abilities to perform well. Positive self-talk lowers anxiety and enhances confidence.

## 5. Visualize Success

Picture yourself successfully finishing the exam with your desired outcome. Visualize confidently answering questions and feeling composed. Visualization helps ease anxiety and fosters a positive mindset.

## 6. Take Care of Yourself

Prioritize your physical and mental well-being during exam prep. Ensure sufficient sleep, a balanced diet, and regular exercise. Your overall health supports stress management and optimal exam performance.

## 7. Seek Support

If exam anxiety becomes overwhelming, seek help from peers, instructors, or a therapist. Talking about your fears provides perspective, while your support network can offer strategies to manage anxiety effectively.

# Practice Tests

## Practice Test 1

**1. When a plausible functional association between a behavior and............ has been established, an analysis of the behavior has been successful.**

A. Environment

B. People

C. Something moveable

✓D. Independent Variable

**2. Uncontrolled factors known or on the other hand thought to apply an effect on the reliant variable are called**

A. Variable

✓ B. Confounding variables

C. Individual Phenomenon

D. Significant Behavior

**3. When a person engages in a behavior, they are exposed to new settings, reinforcers, contingencies, reactions, and stimulus controls, which has immediate and dramatic effects that go far beyond the unique change itself.**

A. Behavioral Management

✓B. Behavioral regulation

C. Mood regulation

D. Behavioral Cusp

**4. An experimental layout in which successive and gradually altering criteria for reinforcement or punishment are used in a series of treatment phases after a baseline phase. The degree to which the level of responding modifies in accordance with each new criterion serves as proof of experimental control.**

A. Codic

✓B. Changing criterion design

C. Aversive stimulus

D. Escape Contingency

**5. Stimuli that lead people to react in overlapping ways, not because they are physically identical, but rather because social-verbal reinforcement contingencies have trained people to do so.**

A. Guardian consent

B. Multielement Design

C. Arbitrary relations

D. Autoclitic

**6. The predictive power of steady state responding enables the behavior analyst to employ a form of inductive logic known as**

A. DRO Reversal Technique

B. Sequence Effect

C. Noncontingent Reinforcement

D. Affirmation of the consequent

**7. When a reaction is promptly followed by a stimulus alteration that raises the likelihood that subsequent instances of the same response will occur.**

A. Reinforcement

B. Positive reinforcement

C. Negative reinforcement

D. Operant conditioning

**8. A rule that permits temporally distant or implausible but potentially substantial consequences to indirectly govern human conduct (i.e., a verbal expression of an antecedent-behavior consequence contingency).**

A. Rule Governed behavior

B. Classical Conditioning

C. Rule of behavior

D. Productive behavior

**9. The following circumstances offer compelling evidence that behavior is guided by rules or under instructional direction rather than as a direct outcome of reinforcement.**

A. There is obvious immediate repercussion for the behavior.

B. The behavior changes without receiving reinforcement is not normal.

C. The response-consequence delay is more than 60 seconds.

D. Following one incidence of reward, there is a significant rise in the frequency of the behavior.

**10. When a behavior persists in the absence of any known reinforce**

A. Positive Reinforcement

B. Negative reinforcement

✓C. Automatic reinforcement

D. Elimination of reinforcement

**11. The terms primary reinforcer and unlearned reinforcer are synonyms for**

A. Measurement of behavior

✓B. Unconditioned Reinforcer

C. Conditioned reinforcer

D. Punishment

**12. The low-occurrence behavior will be reinforced when there is a chance to participate in a behavior that happens at a relatively high free operant (or baseline) rate in response to the occurrence of the low-occurrence behavior. "When you finished your homework you can watch TV," the teacher tells a student who generally spends far more time watching TV than working on their assignments.**

✓A. Premack principle

B. Law of attraction

C. Grandmas law

D. Both AC

**13. A conditioned reinforcer whose effectiveness is not dependent on a present EO for any particular sort of reinforcement because it has been coupled with numerous unconditioned and conditioned reinforcers. For instance, proximity and eye contact during social interactions.**

✓A. Generalized Conditioned Reinforcer

B. Specific Conditioning

C. Negative Evaluation

D. Edible reinforces

**14.** Using the corresponding baseline rates at which every behavior happens and determining whether access to the contingent behavior reflects a restriction in comparison to the baseline level of engagement, a model can be utilized to make a prediction regarding whether or not access to one behavior will act as reinforcement for another behavior (the instrumental response). The prospect of participating in the limited activity is an efficient kind of reinforcement. This is due to the fact that limiting accessibility to a behavior appears to work as an instance of deprivation that serves as an EO.

A. Low-rate target

B. Response deprivation hypothesis

C. Proximity

D. Baseline Conditioning

**15.** Events that frequently operate as reinforcers include physical touch (such as hugs and pats on the back), closeness (such as walking up to, standing next to, or sitting next to a person), attention, and praise. One of the most potent and often successful sources of reinforcement for kids is adult attention. Some behavior analysts have hypothesized that some parts of social attention may involve unconditioned reinforcement due to the almost universal effects of contingent social attention as reward.

A. Tangible reinforcer

B. Social reinforcer

C. Activity reinforcer

D. Sensory reinforce

**16.** Process of acquiring and combining psychological data for psychological evaluation, using case studies, behavioral observation, exams, interviews, and especially created instruments and measurement processes.

A. Measurement

B. Clinical interview

C. Psychological Assessment

D. Behavioral observation

**17.** A measurement is a proportion made up of the dimensions of count (the total number of replies) and time (the duration of the observational period during which the count was gathered).

A. Assessment

B. Rate

C. Count

D. Measurement

**18. Answering a question posed by the teacher, responding to flash cards the teacher has presented, and, when given a sample color, pointing to a color from a group of three that matches the sample color. In each of these instances, the presentation of a discriminative stimulus regulates the rate of response. Because behaviors that occur within**

A. Extended period

B. Free operant

C. Discrete trials

D. Reference the counting number

**19. Multiple occurrences of a behavior throughout time (i.e., conduct that can be counted)**

A. Repeatability

B. Frequency

C. Countability

D. Both A and C

**20. As stated by Thompson and Iwata (2005), the optimal control technique for positive reinforcement eliminates the contingent connection between the occurrence of the desired response and the display of the stimulus, while simultaneously taking into account the influences of**

A. High rate of activity

B. Stimulus presentation

C. Absence of stimulus

D. Continues of stimulation

**21. This technique has at least five stages (ABCBC): A is the initial condition; B is the reinforcement condition, where the possible reinforcer is offered if the target behavior occurs; and C is the alternative behavior condition, where the potential reinforcer is presented if the alternative behavior occurs. The analyst will then repeat phases B and C to see if the level of responding alters in response to the response-consequence contingency being present or absent.**

A. Differential reinforcement of alternative behavior

B. Noncontingent Reinforcement

C. Positive reinforcement

D. DRA and option A

**22. We provide practitioners with nine recommendations for using positive reinforcement successfully. These recommendations originate primarily from three sources:**

A. The study literatures of applied behavior analysis

B. Experimental behavior analysis

C. our own experiences

D. All above

**23. The majority of behavior sustained by negative reinforcement is defined by a process in which a response blocks or delays the presentation of a stimulus, despite the fact that escape scenarios are frequently encountered in ordinary life.**

A. Negative Contingency

B. Escape Contingency

C. Avoidance Contingency

D. Discriminated Avoidance

**24. Even without a signal, avoidance behavior might develop. Let's say the experimenter sets up a timetable where the bright light is activated for 5 seconds every 30 seconds, and any reaction during the interval causes the clock to be reset to zero. This kind of configuration is referred to as**

A. Escape

B. Behavioral observation

C. Discriminated Avoidance

D. Free operant avoidance

**25. A stimulus is a previously neutral event that gains its consequences by being paired with an already-present deterrent reinforcer. Because of the strong correlation between dark clouds and imminent poor weather, a bicyclist, for instance, frequently turns around when they notice a very overcast sky and heads home. Perhaps the most typical conditioned negative reinforcers are different types of social compulsion, such parental nagging.**

A. Conditioned negative reinforcer

B. Automatic negative reinforcement

C. Unconditioned negative reinforcer

D. Automatic positive reinforcement

**26. In general, the following circumstances will lead to greater effectiveness of negative reinforcement for a particular response:**

A. Target response is not occurrence is promptly followed by a change in the stimuli.

B. The amount of reinforcement, or the difference between the stimulation before and after the response, is substantial.

C. The intended response regularly causes escape from or postponement of the EO when it not occurs regularly.

D. Competing responses receive reinforcement.

**27. The development of academic skills may be significantly influenced by negative reinforcement, but it can also be explained by it.**

A. Behavior maintenance

B. Negative reinforcement

C. Disruptive behavior

D. Antecedent Event

**28. Negative reinforcement for a particular action will typically be more powerful when**

A. The stimulus change occurs right after the target response

B. The level of reinforcement is small,

C. The target response don't consistently occurs

D. Reinforcement is accessible for competing responses.

**29. A schedule of reinforcement calls for a reinforcer to finish a predetermined number of answers. Reinforcement is produced after every fourth accurate (or target) response. In order to produce reinforcement, 15 schedule needs 15 replies. Each ratio need was conceived of by Skinner (1938) as a response unit. As a result, rather than merely the final answer of the ratio, the response unit also generates the reinforcer.**

A. Fixed interval schedule

B. Fixed Ratio schedule

C. Consistency of reinforcement

D. Consistency of performance

**30. A timetable for reinforcement requires a certain number of replies to be finished in order to produce a reinforcer. The VR schedule is indicated by a number that corresponds to the mean (or average) number of replies needed for reinforcement. For instance, a 10 schedule often rewards reinforcement for every tenth accurate response. The average number of replies needed for reinforcement is 10, for example, 1 + 14 + 5 + 19 + 11 = 50; 50/5 = 10. Reinforcement can come after a response of l, 14, 5, 19, or n**

A.  Fixed ratio schedule

B. Rate of response

C. Variable ratio schedule

D. None of above

**31. When a behavior takes place in relation to other important events (like the delay between the beginning of an antecedent event and the behavior's occurrence) and the length of time between two successive occurrences of a response class.**

A. Motor Movement

B. Temporal Locus

C. Duration per Occurrence

D. Derivative measures

**32. A measurement of the interval between two occurrences of a behavior in a row. Similar to response latency, a measure of temporal locus since it shows the time relationship between one event and a particular instance of behavior.**

A. Latency

B. Interresponse time IRT

C.  Measure of count

D. Percentage

**33. Not included in stages of psychological assessment**

A. Planning the assessment

B. Data Collection

C. Processing assessment data

D. Norm Referenced test

**34. As woody in 1980 has stated that clinical assessment is individually oriented but it always considers.**

A. personality trait

B. social existence

C. social difference

• D. personality assessment

**35. A legal procedure through which another person the surrogate is authorized to act on behalf of an individual who has been shown to be inept, based on the surrogate's understanding of the incapacitated person's preferences. Most frequently, family members or close friends act as**

A. Inform consent

• B. Surrogate consent

C. Guardian consent

D. Application Form

**36. When it is offered freely, without pressure, duress, or any other improper influence, and when it is provided with the knowledge that it may be revoked at any time. "Consent that is revoked has the same implications as consent that is initially refused."**

A. Voluntary Decision

B. Involuntary Decision

C. Risk benefit analysis

D. Capacity to decide

**37. Multiple stimuli available at once for the brain to choose from A client must have options, be able to execute each option, and be able to feel the natural repercussions of the alternative they choose in order to have a fair decision.**

A. Breach of confidentiality

B. Choice of central principle

• C. Stimulus Alternatives

D. Negative reinforcement

**38.** When one of the main parties, acting alone or jointly with family, friends, or associates, has a personal stake in how the contact turns out. Conflict most frequently manifests itself in dual- or multiple-role partnerships. Conflicts occur when a person working as a therapist establishes another kind of contact with a client, a member of the client's family, or a close friend of the client, or makes a commitment to do so in the future. These connections may be profitable to the therapist in terms of money, relationships, careers, or other factors.

A. Conflict of interest

B. Least restrictive Alternatives

C. Analysis and reaction

D. Behavioral management

**39.** One method of motivation that reduces the ability of a stimulus, thing, or event to act as reinforcement is called a reduction in reinforcement. As an illustration, the act of eating meals removes the capacity of food to promote desirable conduct.

A. Abolishing Operation

B. Antecedent

C. Alternative schedule

D. Accuracy

**40.** Experimentation is used to identify the components that are responsible for socially important behavior, which is the science that involves the utilization of tactics that depend on behavioral principles in order to enhance socially noteworthy conduct.

A. AART

B. ABA

C. ACT

D. AARR

**41.** a method of conducting an experiment that consists of an initial baseline phase until steady state responding is achieved, an initial intervention phase during which the treatment variable is used up until steady state responding is used until the behavior has altered is achieved, the first phase is a return to baseline conditions, during which the independent variable is withdrawn to test whether or not the response "reverses" to the levels that were observed in the first baseline phase. The second phase is an intervention phase to ascertain the outcome.

A. A-B-A-B Design

B. Reversal design

C. Withdrawal Design

D. All Above

**42. A method where some task analysis steps are skipped; used to teach lengthy behavior chains more effectively when there is indication that the omitted steps are already part of the learner's repertoire.**

A. Backward Chaining

B. Chaining

C. Shaping

D. Backward chaining with leaps ahead

**43. A linguistic cusp of higher order in which the repertoires of the speaker and the listener are blended in reciprocal relations. To produce a tact, a new word acquired as a listener may generate a listener relation, and a new word gained as a tact can create a listener relation. This is true even without additional training.**

A. Bidirectional naming

B. Radical behaviorism

C. Pragmatism

D. Observed value

**44. A description of behavior modification employing conditioned reinforcement in the form of an aural stimulus that was made popular by Pryor (1999). When pressed, a portable device makes a clicking noise. The click sound is combined with various forms of reinforcement, like as tasty rewards, by the trainer to make it a conditioned reinforcer.**

A. Clicker Training

B. operant behavior

C. classical conditioning

D. momentary time sampling

**45. Any study that aims to discover the main elements of an intervention, the corresponding roles of different elements inside a treatment plan, or the active components of a therapeutic state is considered to be a type of intervention investigation. Although there are many other types of component analyses, the fundamental technique is to compare the levels of responding throughout each phase of the intervention while leaving out one or more components.**

A. BACB's Professional and Ethical Compliance Code for Behavior Analysts

B. Irreversibility

C. Multiple baseline design

D. joint control

**46.** Any stimulus that is made to function for the desired behavior in the learning environment and later prompts or helps the learner to carry out the desired behavior in a generalization environment.

A. Applied behavioral Assessment

B. Reaction formation

C. Contrived Mediating stimulus

D. General case analysis

**47.** A device that automatically creates records that display response rates in real time; each time a response is emitted, a pen glides upward over paper that is continuously moving at a steady speed.

A. Fixed momentary

B. Cumulative recorder

C. backward chaining

D. Free operant

**48.** A situation in which reinforcement for each member of a group is based on their behavior or the behavior of a small group of individuals inside the larger group.

A. Dependent group contingency

B. Independent contingency

C. Irreversible behavior

D. None of above

**49.** A stimulus that has historically resulted in punishment for a certain behavior while present, but not when it is absent; as a result of this history, the behavior happens less frequently when the SDP is present than when it is not.

A. Concept Formation

B. Celebration

C. Discriminative stimulus for punishment

D. Class merger

**50.** When reactions are made at any point in the period before the aversive stimulus is supposed to appear, this is referred to as a contingency.

A. Free operant Avoidance

B. Verbal Aggression

C. Pretending

D. Communication style

**51. When a previously reinforced behavior is no longer reinforced (i.e., responses no longer do so), the main result is a decline in the frequency of the behavior until it reaches a PR reinforced level or eventually stops happening.**

A. True Value

B. Controlled environment

C. Ratio

D. Extinction

**52. Stimuli that have similar physical characteristics, including having four legs, being round, being blue, or having common related relationships**

A. Feature stimulus class

B. Class expansion

C. Behavioral cusp

D. Prevention method

**53. Occurs when the controlling antecedent stimulus, the response, or the response product (e.g., stimulus and response are both visual, aural, and tactile) share the same sense modality, and (b) physically resemble one another. Echoic, text copying, and imitation in connection to sign language are examples of verbal relations with formal resemblance.**

A. Formal Similarity

B. ABC recording

C. Abative Effect

D. Functional Communication training

**54. The following ethical considerations for applied behavioral analysts:**

A. Moral issues with the employer

B. Ethics of Research Considerations

C. Difficulty in Making Decisions

D. All above

**55. Word-of-mouth marketing is a potent tool for promoting any business or institution, and while it may be very advantageous, it can also be very harmful. It could harm the reputation of the behavior analyst as well as the business or organization if someone feels they are being treated unethically.**

A. Adjunctive Behavior

B. Neural pathway

C. Reputation Damage

D. Ethical consideration

**56. Is not IEP meeting tip**

A. Examine the newly provided documents. Add annotations in the margins.

B. Determine if you want to sign the IEP in person at the meeting. We usually advise reading the IEP at home before signing it.

C. For further information, don't speak with any IEP team member.

D. When contacting school staff, provide the standard 24-hour response time.

**57. A schedule of reinforcement in which a discriminative stimulus is correlated with each element and response requirements of two & more basic schedules must be satisfied in a certain order before reward is supplied.**

A. Contingent

B. Chained Schedule

C. Negative reinforcement

D. Effective training

**58. Few people are interested in dealing with litigation, whether it be on an individual or organizational basis. Every Behavior Analyst must behave in accordance with the highest ethical standards that have been laid forth for them in order to prevent legal action.**

A. Cumulative record

B. Litigation

C. Punishment

D. Space analysis

**59.** Behavioral techniques to teach rats to push a bar that releases food pellets, for example. Any progress they made until they achieved that goal was rewarded with a pellet. The animals practiced the task until they perfected it

A. Behaviorist

B. Freudian

C. Aron Beck

D. B.F Skinner

**60.** In order to treat autistic children, Loaves established the Young Autism Project at the University of California, Los Angeles. The project developed the strategies and objectives that eventually led to ABA. The goal was to make the child as "normal" as possible by teaching them actions like hugging and maintaining eye contact for a prolonged amount of time, both of which are avoided by autistic children and make them stand out.

A. In 1966

B. 1985

C. In 1887

D. In 1970

**61.** When the start, middle, and end of the verbal stimulus and the start, middle, and end of the verbal re the same, there is a relationship between the two. The verbal relationships associated with point-to-point communication include echoic, text copying, imitation of sign language, textual, and transcription.

A. Assertiveness

B. Point to point correspondence

C. Denial

D. Feature stimulus class

**62.** A branch of behaviorism that seeks to explain all human behavior, including private occurrences like thoughts and feelings, in terms of influencing factors in the person's and species' evolutionary history (phylogeny).

A. Descending baseline

B. ABC

C. Radical Behaviorism

D. Stimulus

**63. A two-dimensional graph with a logarithmically scaled y axis, where similar vertical distances imply proportionally equivalent changes in behavior.**

A. Memory

B. Semilogarithmic chart

C. DBT

D. Accuracy of measurement

**64. An antecedent stimulus, a behavior, and a consequence are all included in the basic unit of analysis that makes up an analysis of operant behavior.**

A. Contingency

B. Cognitive Error

C. Three term contingency

D. Trial and Error

**65. To investigate sensory equivalence and conditional links, a discrete trial methodology is utilized. The beginning of a matching-to-sample trial is marked by an initial reaction that either presents or exposes the sample stimulus of interest. Following this, the sample stimulus may or may not be removed, and two or more comparison stimuli may or may not be displayed. The next step is for the participant to choose which comparative stimulus to employ. Responses that select a comparison stimulus that is identical to the sample stimulus are rewarded with reinforcement, whereas responses that select comparison stimuli that are not identical to the sample stimulus are not rewarded with reinforcement.**

A. Matching law

B. Matching to sample procedure

C. Multipipeline across normal design

D. Multielement Design

**66. A method for altering behavior in which students learn new skills by mimicking the skills being displayed by real or imagined models. The learner's intended conduct is explicitly shown, shown, or communicated by the model. Models might be actual performances or figurative depictions of the intended behavior.**

A. Chaining

B. Prompting

C. Modeling

D. Reinforcement

**67. A state that frequently obstructs learning and has a very narrow range of discriminative stimuli, or stimulus features controlling behavior.**

A. Over selective stimulus control

B. Behavioral Assessment

C. Measurement

D. All above

**68. A tact elicited by a new stimulus that shares some of the important characteristics of the original stimulus but not all of them.**

A. Pivotal behavior

B. Classical conditioning

C. Metaphorical extension

D. Extinction

**69. Any experimental design that compares the effects of two or more experimental conditions to the baseline and/or to one another using the experimental techniques and logic of the reversal tactic.**

(For instance, A-8-A-8-C-8-C, A-8-A-C-A-D-A-C-A, and A-8-A-8-8 +C-8 -8+C).

A. Methodological Behaviorism

B. Learning

C. Defense mechanism

D. Multiple treatment reversal design

**70. There are two interpretations of this phrase in applied behavior analysis:**

(a) The extent to which the learner continues to exhibit the target behavior following the completion of all or part of the intervention a behavioral trait or dependent variable

(b) A condition for which treatment has been stopped altogether or only in part, an independent variable, or an experimental circumstance.

A. Maintenance

B. Magnitude

C. Massed practice

D. Mand

**71. A situation where another person presents the stimulus for the behavior's antecedent and/or its outcome.**

A. External validity

B. Generalized Imitation

C. Socially mediated contingency

D. Frequency

**72. A reinforcement schedule that offers reinforcement for the first right after the passing of various amounts of time that happen in a random or unpredictable order. On a VI IO-min schedule, reinforcement is supplied for the initial response after an average of Io minutes have passed since the last reinforced response, although the amount of time that has passed since the last reinforced response may range from 30 seconds or less to 25 minutes or more.**

A. Discrete Trial

B. Variable interval

C. Fading

D. Explanatory Fiction

**73. According to a theory of derived stimulus relations, broad repertoires of relating are created as a result of cumulative experience with relational exemplars and the idea that stimulus interactions are linguistic by nature.**

A. Functional Analysis

B. Full session DRL

C. Relational frame theory

D. Environment

**74. The absence of response for some time after reinforcement; this effect is frequently brought on by fixed interval (Fl) and fixed ratio (FR) reinforcement regimens.**

A. Confidentiality

B. Post reinforcement pause

C. Punishment

D. Direct measurement

**75. A range of techniques used to identify the stimuli that an individual favors, their relative preference values (high versus low), the circumstances in which those preference values persist, and their alleged value as reinforcers.**

A. Determinism

B. inform consent

C. Stimulus preference assessment

D. Consequences

**76. A setup where different sensory equivalence probes are provided in order, first with symmetry, then transitivity and finally a combined test**

A. Descending baseline

B. simple-to-complex testing protocol A

C. Constant delay

D. Replication

**77. A two-dimensional graph that displays the relative placement of several measurements within a data collection in relation to the x- and y-axis-depicted variables A scatterplot has unconnected data points.**

A. Bonus response cost

B. ABA

C. APA

D. Scatterplot

**78. A multiply-divide graph with six base-lO (or x I o,., 10) cycles on the vertical axis that can handle response rates between 0.000695 per minute and 1000 per minute. It makes it possible to standardize the charting of celebration, a factor that determines how much behavior is multiplied or divided by time per unit.**

A. High probability

B. Prompting

C. Chaining

D. Standard celebration chart

**79. An anxiety, fear, or phobia treatment using behavior therapy that includes replacing the anxious or fearful behavior with a desired reaction, usually muscle relaxation. The client exercises relaxation while visualizing anxiety-inducing scenarios in a progression from the least frightening to the most frightening**

A. Habilitation

B. interval variable

C. Systematic Desensitization

D. Good behavior game

**80. A measurement of the behavior's existence or absence over a period of time. It works best with consistent, rapid behaviors. (See also whole-interval recording, partial-interval recording, and brief time sampling.)**

A. Time Sampling

B. Modeling

C. Learned behavior

D. Imitation

**81. A type of verbal behaviour in which the speaker's distinctive response topography has an impact on the listener; comprises (e.g., speech, sign language, writing, fingerspelling).**

A. Reversible reaction

B. Topography based verbal behavior

C. Impure Tact

D. Independent group

**82. An environmental factor that, as a result of learning history, establishes (or eliminates) the effectiveness of another stimulus's reinforcement and elicits (or suppresses) the behavior that other stimulus-reinforced.**

A. internal validity

B. External pressure

C. Transitive conditioned motivating operation

D. Hero procedure

**83.** A more conservative and useful JOA index for discrete trial data than the total count IOA is produced by comparing the observers' counts on an item-by-item or trial-by-trial basis.

A. Trial by trial IOA

B. Intraverbal control

C. Listener Discrimination

D. Maintenance

**84.** A false positive is when a researcher assumes there is a relationship between the independent and dependent variables when there isn't one.

A. Line graph

B. Type I error

C. Limited hole

D. Level

**85.** A technique for evaluating behavior via time sampling in which the observation period is split up into a series of short time intervals (typically from 5 to 15 seconds). The observer reports whether the target behavior persisted through the full interval at the conclusion of each interval; this practice has the tendency to underestimate the total proportion of the observation time during which the target behaviors actually happened.

A. Magnitude

B. Messed practice

C. Whole interval recording

D. Latency

## Answer Key

| | | |
|---|---|---|
| 1.  A | 11. B | 21. D |
| 2.  B | 12. D | 22. D |
| 3.  D | 13. A | 23. C |
| 4.  B | 14. B | 24. D |
| 5.  C | 15. B | 25. A |
| 6.  D | 16. C | 26. B |
| 7.  B | 17. B | 27. C |
| 8.  A | 18. C | 28. A |
| 9.  D | 19. D | 29. B |
| 10. C | 20. B | 30. C |

| | | |
|---|---|---|
| 31. B | 50. A | 69. D |
| 32. B | 51. D | 70. A |
| 33. D | 52. A | 71. C |
| 34. B | 53. A | 72. B |
| 35. B | 54. D | 73. C |
| 36. A | 55. C | 74. B |
| 37. C | 56. C | 75. C |
| 38. A | 57. B | 76. B |
| 39. A | 58. B | 77. D |
| 40. B | 59. D | 78. D |
| 41. D | 60. D | 79. C |
| 42. D | 61. B | 80. A |
| 43. A | 62. C | 81. B |
| 44. A | 63. B | 82. C |
| 45. A | 64. C | 83. A |
| 46. C | 65. B | 84. B |
| 47. B | 66. C | 85. C |
| 48. A | 67. A | |
| 49. C | 68. C | |

# Practice Test 2

**1. Any individual who is contemplating the provision of services or participation in research should be provided with information in language that is straightforward and uncomplicated regarding all of the significant aspects of the planned treatment, all of the possible hazards and advantages of the planned procedure, all of the potential alternative treatments, and the right to refuse continued treatment at any time. The all information is**

A. Baseline behavior

B. Reinforcement

C. Ethical compliance code for behavioral analyst ✓

D. Knowledge about treatment

**2. When it is offered freely, without pressure, duress, or any other improper influence, and when it is provided with the knowledge that it may be revoked at any time. Revocation of permission has the same consequences as an original denial to consent, according to Yell (1998).**

A. Affirmation of the consequence

B. Autoclitic

C. Voluntary Decision ✓

D. None of above

**3. When someone is being abused or when there is knowledge of potential damage to them or to others, confidentiality is not guaranteed. In all states, professionals are required to report any suspicion of child abuse, and in the majority of states, suspicion of elder abuse is.**

A. Artifact

B. Limit of confidentiality      *B*

C. Behavior

D. BACB professional ✓

**4. Breach of confidentiality occurs due to following reasons**

A. The breach is done on purpose to keep someone safe.

B. The violation was unintended and came about as a result of negligence, carelessness, or an incorrect understanding of confidentiality.

C. Behavioral analysis

D. Both AB ✓

**5. The duty to safeguard a client's safety, health, and dignity. A number of rights, such as the right to privacy, the right to a therapeutic treatment setting, and the freedom to refuse treatment, must be respected and safeguarded.**

A. Practicing ABA analyst ✓

B. Aversive checklist

C. Behavioral chain

D. BAB Design

**6. Codes that provide recommendations for association members to take into account when making decisions or carrying out their professional responsibilities. Additionally, these principles offer the benchmark by which graduated consequences for breaking the code can be applied (e.g., reprimand, censure, expulsion from the organization).**

A. Interrupted Chain procedure

B. Magnitude

C. Ethical codes of behavior ✓

D. Joint Control


**7. When one of the main parties, acting alone or jointly with family, friends, or associates, has a personal stake in how the contact turns out. Dual role relationships are where the majority of conflict occurs.**

A. Irreversibility

B. External Validity

C. Conflict of interest ✓

D. Local response rate


**8. Before any evaluation or treatment is given, the prospective client for services or participant in a research study explicitly consents. Getting permission is only the first step toward informed consent. After the participant has received complete disclosure and information, permission must follow.**

A. Undertaking

B. Informed Consent ✓

C. Guardian consent

D. Confidentiality


**9. A legal procedure wherein another person is able to act on someone else's behalf who has been determined to be incompetent based on knowledge of what the incapacitated person would have preferred. The most frequent surrogates are members of the family or close friends.**

A. Multiple behavior

B. Law enforcement

C. Surrogate Consent ✓

D. Critical analysis

10. Three essential and fundamentally important behaviors, actions, and decisions are: What is the appropriate thing to do? What should one endeavor? What exactly does a competent behavior analyst entail? Smith, Reich, 1988 These questions serve as a guide for doing both personal and professional practices, which are primarily undertaken with the aim of assisting others in bettering their physical, social, psychological, familial, or personal circumstances. The primary goal of ethical practice, according to Corey, Corey, and Callanan (1993), is to advance the welfare of the client.

A. Rate too low

B. Term refer as Ethics

C. Discriminable contingency

D. Duration too brief

11. a range of techniques used to identify the stimuli that the person prefers, their relative preference values (high preference versus low preference), and the circumstances in which those preference values change as task demands, deprivation situations, or reinforcement schedules are altered

A. Program common stimuli

B. Stimulus preference assessment

C. Multiple exemplar training

D. General case analysis

12. A good illustration of the impact of instructors' social reinforcement on preschool children's cooperative play is seen in Baer and Wolf's (1970a) study.

A. Cue cards

B. NCR reversal technique

C. Delayed Rewards

D. Visual activity schedule

13. The researcher draws the incorrect conclusion that an independent variable had no impact on the dependent variable. Ideally, a researcher will properly conclude that there is a functional relation between the independent and dependent variables by employing well-justified experimental strategies, competent experimental design, and acceptable methods of data analysis.

A. Trial and error

B. Type II error

C. Mistaken behavior

D. None of above

14. Depending on whether or not access to the contingent activity constitutes a constraint in comparison to the baseline level of participation and the relative baseline rates at which each action happens, the following are some important considerations, a model can be used to predict whether one behavior will act as reinforcement for another behavior. Possibility of engaging in the restricted activity is an effective kind of reinforcement since restricting access to a behavior apparently functions as a form of deprivation that serves as an EO.

A. Response in behavior

B. Response deprivation hypothesis

C. Naïve observer

D. Measurement error

15. Taking action when a signal is present delays the occurrence of a stimulus from which escape is a reinforcer. The tone is a discriminative stimulus (SD) that increases the possibility of responding reinforcement because responses in the presence of the tone are reinforced whereas responses in the absence of the tone have no impact.

A. Tact extinction

B. Discriminated Avoidance

C. Mean count per interval

D. Verbal communication

16. When coupled with an existing (unconditioned or conditioned) negative reinforcer, produce effects that were previously neutral. If the sky is substantially clouded, a bicyclist will typically turn around and ride home because of the strong correlation between dark clouds and inclement weather. Perhaps the most typical conditioned negative reinforcers are different types of social compulsion, such parental nagging.

A. unconditioned punisher

B. Practice Effect

C. Conditioned negative reinforcers

D. Radical behaviorism

17. The consequences of a subject's prior experience with a condition on how they behave in a current situation. For instance, care must be taken when interpreting the outcomes of the A-B-C-B-C design that arise from the rather typical series of occurrences in real-world applications.

A. Prediction

B. Sequence Effects

C. Reactivity

D. Phylogeny

**18. Each instance of behavior takes place in relation to other events at a specific time (i.e., when behavior occurs can be measured).**

A. Temporal locus

B. Precision teaching

C. Ratio Scale

D. All above

**19. Reversal experiments compare the outcomes of two or more experimental conditions to the control condition and/or to one another.**

A. Responds conditioning

B. Multiple treatment reversal design

C. Behavioral issues

D. Rate

**20. Establishing and/or maintaining personal habits that are as culturally acceptable as feasible by the use of increasingly more typical settings, expectations, and processes. The goal of obtaining the greatest physical and social integration of people with disabilities into society's mainstream is not one technique, but rather a philosophical perspective.**

A. Higher order conditioning

B. Normalization

C. Response set

D. Reflex

**21. The degree to which a measurement method produces the same result when used repeatedly to gauge the same aspect of nature**

A. Reliability

B. Account

C. Validity

D. Confidentiality

**22. When an observer is aware that other people are analyzing the data he reports, measurement inaccuracy occurs.**

A. Denial

B. Applied behavior

C. Observer reactivity

D. Mutual entailment

**23.** The term "disagreement" refers to any instance in which one observer reported that the behavior did not occur while the other observer observed that it did occur. For the sake of this discussion, an agreement is deemed to be present when both observers documented the absence of the behavior within the same interval.

A. Unscored interval IOA

B. Measurement by permanent product

C. Verbal behavior

D. Operant behavior

**24.** The degree to which two or more independent observers who conducted measurements of the identical events report the same values that they have observed. There is a wide variety of approaches to estimate IOA, and each of these approaches provides a somewhat unique viewpoint on the degree of agreement and disagreement that exists amongst observers.

A. Classical conditioning

B. Mixed Schedule

C. Molt

D. Interobserver Agreement

**25.** The intensity of the antecedent event (EO) that causes behavior gives rise to ethical questions concerning the use of positive and negative reinforcement that are related. Aversive events can be considered the majority of EOs for behavior that is maintained by negative reinforcement. When offered as preceding stimuli, extremely unpleasant occurrences cannot be explained as

A. Momentary time sampling

B. Modeling

C. Typical behavior change program

D. None of above

**26. Multiple occurrences of a response class are possible through time (i.e., conduct can be counted) (i.e., behavior can be counted)**

A. Repeatability

B. Observer drift

C. Contrived contingency

D. Mentalism

27. A lot of data is obtained about the individual and the numerous settings in which they reside and work. Physiological circumstances, physical characteristics of the environment (such as lighting, seating arrangements, noise level), interactions with people, one's home environment, and past reinforcement history are just a few of the numerous variables that can influence a person's behavior. Each of these elements is a potential area for evaluation.

A. Observer reactivity

B. Ecological Assessment ✓

C. Multiple probe design

D. Most to least response prompt

28. A measurable and modifiable aspect of behavior is the physical form or shape of a behavior. Measured amount of behavior due to the ability to distinguish one response from another when it takes on different forms. The fact that reactions of various forms are formed and chosen by their consequences shows that is a flexible component of behavior.

A. Manipulation

B. Topography ✓

C. Behavioral management

D. Ontogeny

29. A change in the stimulus that, when applied without any prior matching with punishment, can reduce the frequency of any behavior that comes before it in the future.

A. Level system

B. Interresponse time

C. Unconditioned Punisher

D. Contingency ✓

30. The amount of time between two instances of the same answer type that occur back-to-back. IRT like reaction latency, is a measure of temporal locus since it shows how soon after an event in this case, the prior response—a particular instance of behavior happens.

A. Interresponse time ✓

B. Unscored interval IOA

C. Limited hold

D. All above

**31. Desk calendar VR Process is not**

A. Desk calendars with loose-leaf date pages attached to the base are given to students.

B. The instructor takes the date pages off the calendar's foundation. ✓

C. The instructor not decides on the pupils' maximum ratio.

D. From 1 to the maximum ratio, the teacher sequentially numbers the index cards.

**32. The preferred strategy for choosing which behaviors to target for change is to make direct and frequent observations of the client's behavior in a natural setting. Bijou, Peterson, and Ault (1968) introduced the term "basic kind of direct continuous observation" to describe this type of observation.**

A. Option D

B. Anecdotal observation

C. Learning behavior ✓

D. Punisher

**33. Measurement done in a way that ensures all instances of the relevant response classes are found throughout the observation period**

A. Continues measurement ✓

B. Hypothetical contrast

C. Imitation

D. Instructional setting

**34. The extent to which a person's repertoire maximizes short- and long-term rewards for themselves and others while minimizing short- and long-term punishments**

A. Generalization setting ✓

B. Habilitation

C. Punishment

D. Function based definition

**35. Nonrandom measurement error is a type of measurement error that is more likely to go in one direction than another. It is equally likely to overstate an event's true value as it is to underestimate it when measurement inaccuracy is random. The reason for this was that John, Tim, and Bill repeatedly overestimated the number of kilometers they had actually travelled.**

A. Measurement Bias

B. History of reinforcement

C. Fixed interval

D. All above

36. When the number of responses is below a criterion that is gradually reduced across time intervals based on the individual's performance (e.g., fewer than five responses per five minutes, fewer than four responses per five minutes, fewer than three responses per five minutes, etc.), the schedule offers reinforcement at the end of the predetermined time interval.

A. Functional analysis

B. Good behavior game

C. Generating Learning

D. Differential reinforcement of diminishing rates ✓

37. Whether the behavior took place at any point throughout the timeframe is noted by the observer. The only thing that matters in partial-interval time sampling is that the behavior happened at some point during the interval, not how often it happened or for how long. Even if the target behavior happens more than once within the interval, it is still only given one point.

A. Partial interval recording ✓

B. Direct measurement

C. Ethical code of behavior

D. Event recording

38. A range of techniques, such as direct observation, interviews, checklists, and tests, are used to define and identify the behavior change targets. In addition to identifying the behavior(s) that require to be shifted, comprehensive behavioral assessments additionally pinpoint the resources, assets, significant others, battling unforeseen circumstances, upkeep and generalization factors, and potential reinforcers and/or punishments that might be utilized in intervention plans to alter the behavior that is being targeted.

A. Errorless learning

B. Duplic

C. Behavioral Assessment ✓

D. Echoic

39. A measurement of the quantity of response opportunities required to reach a particular performance level. The characteristics of the target behavior and the required performance level determine what exactly qualifies as a trial. Trials-to-criterion data are presented as the number of trials necessary for the learner to tie a shoe correctly without prompts or assistance. For a skill like shoe tying, each opportunity to tie a shoe might be considered a trial.

A. Distinction relation

B. Trials to criterion ✓

C. Differential reinforcement of low rates

D. Double blind control

**40.** VR scheduling result in predictable, constant reaction rates. Unlike FR schedules, they often do not cause a post-reinforcement hiatus. The lack of knowledge about the timing of when the subsequent response will result in reinforcement may be the cause of the lack of reaction pauses. Because the following response might result in reinforcement, responding must remain consistent.

A. Learned behavior

B. Consistency of performance

C. Competency to learn

D. Backward Chaining

**41.** The cessation of an existing stimulus (or a lowering of an existing stimulus's intensity) soon after a behavior that causes a reduction in the behavior's future frequency. The participant at the beach party who ignored his food was harshly penalized when a seagull took it away in flight. A "motivating operation for the reinforcer must be in effect, otherwise removing it will not constitute punishment," according to the theory, for a stimulus change to serve as negative punishment, which entails the removal of a positive reinforcer.

A. Procedural Fidelity

B. Tip of Tongue

C. Negative punishment

D. Contrast

**42.** The behavior analyst can use a form of inductive logic because of steady state responding's ability to forecast outcomes.

A. Professional certification of ABA therapist

B. Counter control

C. Social validity

D. Affirmation of the consequent

**43.** "The expected result of a currently undetermined or upcoming measurement. It is the most tasteful use of quantification, and it serves as the foundation for all scientific and technological activity.

A. Capacity to decide

B. Prediction

C. Professional reading

D. Ethical issues

**44. A type of discipline when a wrong behavior results in the loss of a certain amount of reward, it makes it less likely that action will be repeated in future.**

A. Negligence

B. risk benefit analysis

C. Response Cost ✓

D. Voluntary decision

**45. The phrase describes graphs with a single proportionally sized axis.**

A. Alternative Treatment

B. Logarithmic Chart ✓

C. AB design

D. ABA analyst

**46. It is the main focus of consideration in the interpretation and analysis of graphed data because it indicates the degree and pattern of behavior between succeeding data points. The data route represents an approximation of the actual course taken by the behavior during the interval between the two measures because behavior is rarely seen and continuously recorded in applied behavior analysis. The higher the number of measurements and data points produced per unit of time.**

A. Part of measurement

B. Extinction

C. Data Path ✓

D. Behavioral management

**47. a range of direct, data-based techniques that offer one or more stimuli in exchange for a goal response before tracking the impact over time on response rate. Researchers and practitioners have created reinforcer assessment methods to evaluate the comparative effectiveness of various reinforcers for a given behavior under particular circumstances and to ascertain the relative effects of a given stimulus as reinforcement under various and changing conditions**

A. Compliance code

B. Distinct relation

C. Reinforcer assessment

D. All above ✓

**48. A challenging instance of stimulus control requiring both stimulus identification within a class of stimuli and generalization within that class.**

A. Concept Formation

B. Celebration

C. Deprivation

D. Bidirectional naming

**49. As a result of the delivery of response-contingent punishment in the presence of the stimulus, an SDP is defined as a stimulus situation in which a response has a lower likelihood of occurring than it does in its absence.**

A. Ascending baseline

B. Discriminative stimulus for punishment

C. Words discrimination

D. Abolishing behavior

**50. When a systematic replication successfully duplicates the findings of prior research, it not only proves the correctness of those earlier conclusions and increases their external validity by demonstrating that the same effect may be attained under many circumstances. Any element of a previous experiment can be changed in a systematic replication, including the subjects, the environment, how the independent variable is administered, and the goal behaviors.**

A. Frequency

B. Systematic Replication

C. Errorless learning

D. Differential reinforcement

**51. Depending on the problem conduct, the learner is needed to undo the harm the problem behavior produced by restoring the environment to its previous state and then to engage in additional behavior that significantly improves the environment from what it was before the misbehavior.**

A. Exclusion timeout

B. Full session DRL

C. restitution Al Overreaction

D. Option A

**52. The person stays in the time-in environment, but a cubicle, wall, or other similar structure limits his ability to see some areas of the environment.**

A. Equivalence test

B. Event recording

C. Partition time out

D. All above ·

**53. A visual representation of the relative distribution of various measurements within a data set in relation to the variables shown by the x and y axes. The data on this are unrelated.**

A. Generalization training

B. Formal Chaining

C. Scatterplots

D. Fraudulent conduct

**54. Because humans have the innate ability to respond to them or their effects have been established through prior learning, negative reinforcers have an effect on behavior. In the absence of prior knowledge, stimuli that are removed strengthen behavior include**

A. Metonymical extension

B. Unconditioned Negative reinforcement

C. Neutral stimulus

D. Local response rate

**55. When planning an experiment and later when examining the actual data from an ongoing study, the investigator must always be on the lookout for risks to internal validity. The following uncontrolled variables are recognized as having an impact on the dependent variable:**

A. Matching law

B. Confounding Variables

C. Establishing operation

D. Contingency

**56. Exposing a subject to a condition repeatedly while attempting to remove or regulate any outside influences on the behavior and creating a consistent pattern of behavior before introducing the next condition**

A. Cognitive Error

B. Steady state strategy

C. Applied Behavioral Analysis

D. None of above

**57.** There is a common propensity for similar stimuli to likewise evoke a response when an antecedent stimulus has a history of evoking one that has been reinforced in its presence. Stimuli that have similar physical characteristics to the regulating antecedent stimulus trigger this evocative function.

A. Lag reinforcement Schedule

B. Stimulus generalization ✓

C. Irreversibility

D. Mand

**58.** A cap is established by the teacher for each student or group. The chances of failing to meet the contingency increase with increasing maximum number selection. The procedure is

A. Limited hold

B. Interval DRL

C. Tic-Tac-Toe VR Procedure

D. Hero procedure

**59.** Studies are deemed to have a high degree of confidence when they demonstrate with certainty that behavioral changes are dependent on the independent variable rather than of uncontrolled or unknown variables.

A. impure tact

B. Instructional setting

C. Internal Validity ✓

D. independent variable

**60.** The measurement of two or more behaviors displayed by a single subject at the same time. The researcher adds the independent variable to one of the behaviors after steady state response has been achieved under baseline conditions, while keeping baseline conditions for the other activity (s). Once the first behavior has reached steady state or criterion-level performance, the independent variable is applied to the second behavior, and so on.

A. Forward chaining ✓

B. Appropriate behavior

C. Multiple baselines across behavior design

D. Higher operant order class

**61. Colleagues, and Williams earlier described the characteristics of performance on concurrent schedules, and these traits are congruent with the connections formalized by Herrnstein (1961, 1970) as the**

A. Topography

B. Matching Law

C. Terminal behavior

D. Chained schedule ✓

**62. More accurate than the freehand method and considerably quicker than linear regression techniques are a way of computing and drawing lines of progress.**

A. Motivating operation

B. Value altering effect

C. Verbal cues

D. Split line of progress ✓

**63. Reinforcers include things like stickers, trinkets, educational materials, trading cards, and little toys. An object's intrinsic value has no bearing on whether or not it will ultimately be effective as a reinforcer. Almost anything can be used as a reinforcer. These reinforcers are**

A. Verbal time schedule

B. True value

C. Tangible reinforcers ✓

D. Verbal functioning altering effect

**64. Performance gains brought about by opportunities to emit the behavior again so that a baseline assessment can be made.**

A. Video learning

B. Mixed Schedule

C. Practice Effects

D. All of these ✓

**65. Certain configuration of variables in a study that enables accurate comparisons of the effects of the independent variable's presence, absence, or various values. There are countless ways to introduce, remove, change the value of, or combine independent variables across behaviors, environments, and/or subjects.**

A. Self-modeling

B. Trial to control

C. Experimental design ✓

D. Verbal episode

**66.** The formula below illustrates how to compute the percentage of agreement between the total number of replies recorded by two observers by dividing the smaller of the two counts by the bigger count and multiplying by 100:

Smaller count larger count x 100 = total count IOA %

A. Simple discrimination

B. Total count IOA

C. Tact extension

D. Response Class

**67. Food restriction and unpleasant stimulation are referred to as**

A. Whole interval recording

B. Unconditioned motivating operation

C. Textual

D. Simple to complex testing protocol

**68.** The offering of a possible reinforcer on a fixed-time (FT) or flexible time schedule without waiting for the goal behavior to take place. While allowing for the detection of any effects of the stimulus presentation alone, the response-independent presentation of the prospective reinforcer eliminates the contingent relationship between the goal behavior and the stimulus presentation.

A. Science

B. Three delay

C. Flooding

D. Noncontingent reinforcement

**69.** It has been demonstrated that preventing or "blocking" the completion of several problem behaviors, such as chronic hand-mouthing, eye-poking, and pica, by physically acting as soon as the individual starts to emit them can reduce their frequency.

A. Stimulus delta

B. Time sampling

C. Response blocking

D. Option B

**70. A reduction in the frequency of behavior that has been reinforced by a stimulus, object, or event, also known as an**

A. Token economy

B. Abative Effect ✓

C. Momentary

D. Systematic Desensitization

**71. How much of the independent variable is used or carried out planned is**

A. Repeatability

B. Transcription ✓

C. Conditioned Punisher

D. Procedural fidelity

**72. Equivalence is the term used to describe the emergence of appropriate responses to untrained and unreinforced stimulus-stimulus relations after some stimulus-stimulus connections have been reinforced. Behaviorists specify as**

A. Conditioned reflex

B. Temporal extent

C. Stimulus equivalence ✓

D. Unpairing

**73. As a colored wristband that is applied to a child and used as a distinction for rewards**

A. Total count

B. Time out ribbon        B

C. Treatment Drift ✓

D. Task analysis

**74. A stimulus modification that serves as reinforcement even when the learner has no prior experience with it is referred to as an**

A. Thought Stopping

B. Unconditioned Reinforcer ✓

C. Defense mechanism

D. Taking dictation

**75. Creating a series of sequentially organized stages or tasks by breaking a complex skill down into smaller, teachable components.**

A. Response prompt

B. Task analysis ✓

C. Control environment

D. Selection by consequence

**76. When a response will choose a stimulus that matches itself in the absence of training and reinforcement is**

A. Response deprivation hypothesis

B. Overreaction

C. Positive practice

D. Reflexivity ✓

**77. A technique for examining how the independent variable and the acquisition of consecutive approximations or task sequences relate. The multiple probe design allows for the basis for assessing whether behavior change has taken place prior to intervention, as opposed to the multiple baseline design, which collects data concurrently during the initial stage for each person, environment, or behavior in the experiment.**

A. Experimental conditioning

B. Replication

C. Multiple probe design

D. Self-contract

**78. Delivering a reinforcer after a response that was followed by progressively longer silence periods decreased the total response rate. This process of using reinforcement in this way as an intervention to lessen the occurrences of a target behavior is known as**

A. Modeling

B. Differential reinforcement at low rates ✓

C. Shaping

D. All above

**79.** A method based on science that uses rewards to change behavior. A metal tab on the clicker, a portable device, makes a click sound when it is pressed.

A. Sequence Effect

B. Modeling

C. Clicker Training

D. Chaining Process

**80.** A stimulus, item, or event's ability to reinforce behavior is increased, in which case the MO is an establishing operation (EO), or its ability to reinforce behavior is decreased. Hence the MO is an abrogation operation (AO).

A. Impulse analysis

B. Value altering effect

C. Selectionism

D. Restraint

**81.** From delivery to delivery, the time interval for presenting these stimuli stays constant. The NCR time period is programmed by applied behavior analysts to change from delivery to delivery, and this is known as a

A. Interval by interval

B. Variable time schedule

C. Topography based verbal behavior

D. None of these

**82.** The foundation for comparing the effects of two or more independent variables or performing a study can also be provided by experimental designs that incorporate numerous baselines, reversal, and/or alternating treatments methods

A. restitution Al overreaction

B. Prediction

C. Component Analysis

D. Verification

**83.** It will serve as reinforcement for the low-frequency activity to make the opportunity to engage in a behavior that happens at a relatively high free operant (or baseline) rate dependent on the occurrence of the low-frequency behavior. A contingency predicated on the assumption that a student will typically spend significantly more time watching TV than doing schoolwork

A. Premack principle

B. Symmetry

C. Transitivity

D. Newton's law

**84.** The majority of behavior sustained by negative reinforcement is defined by scenarios involving escape, which are frequently experienced in daily life (e.g., we turn off loud noises, shield our eyes from the sun, or flee from an assailant).

A. Negative reinforcement

B. Avoidance contingency

C. Response blocking

D. Relational frame

**85. The Alternating Treatments Design Has Some Benefits**

A. Minimizes the irreversibility issue.

B. Reduces the effects of sequences.

C. Can be applied to erratic data patterns.

D. All Above

## Answer Key

| | | | | | |
|---|---|---|---|---|---|
| 1. | D | 11. | B | 21. | A |
| 2. | C | 12. | B | 22. | C |
| 3. | B | 13. | B | 23. | A |
| 4. | D | 14. | B | 24. | D |
| 5. | A | 15. | B | 25. | C |
| 6. | C | 16. | C | 26. | A |
| 7. | C | 17. | B | 27. | B |
| 8. | B | 18. | A | 28. | B |
| 9. | C | 19. | B | 29. | C |
| 10. | B | 20. | B | 30. | A |

| 31. C | 50. B | 69. C |
|---|---|---|
| 32. B | 51. C | 70. B |
| 33. A | 52. C | 71. D |
| 34. B | 53. C | 72. C |
| 35. A | 54. B | 73. B |
| 36. D | 55. B | 74. B |
| 37. A | 56. B | 75. B |
| 38. C | 57. B | 76. D |
| 39. B | 58. C | 77. C |
| 40. B | 59. C | 78. B |
| 41. C | 60. C | 79. C |
| 42. D | 61. B | 80. B |
| 43. B | 62. D | 81. B |
| 44. C | 63. C | 82. C |
| 45. B | 64. C | 83. A |
| 46. C | 65. C | 84. B |
| 47. C | 66. B | 85. D |
| 48. A | 67. B | |
| 49. B | 68. D | |

# Practice Test 3

**1. The relation between the behavior and its determining variable is expressed as a function?**

A. x=f(y)

B. y=f(x)

C. x=f(t)

D. y=f(t)

**2. A functional relation exists when a well-controlled experiment reveals the specific change in one event that is _____ variable, which can reliably be produced by specific manipulations of another event that is _____variable.**

A. Independent, dependent

B. Independent, Independent

C. Dependent, independent

D. Dependent, dependent

**3. The most valid and preferred type of data collection is_____.**

A. Continuous measurements.

B. Discontinuous measurements.

C. Conditioned reinforce

D. Response generalization.

**4. John is keeping track of a client's actions. When the customer starts shouting, he starts the stopwatch and stops it when the client stops shouting. What kind of measurement method is he employing?**

A. Frequency

B. Duration

C. Rate

D. IRT

**5. An RBT reported a percentage of data collection with occurrence as his data collection. He is using _____ method.**

A. Partial interval

B. Interval data

C. Whole interval

D. Momentary time sampling

**6. You must record the number of verbal refusals your client makes throughout the course of 45-minute intervals, according to your BCBA's instructions. What method of data gathering would you use?**

A. Frequency

B. Count

C. Rate

D. Partial interval recording

**7. Your BCBA instructs you to take frequent and short data. What is the best type of measurement to use?**

A. Partial interval

B. Duration

C. Frequency

D. Latency

**8. As an RBT, you want a quick and easy way to record five different students' task engagement. What should be the preferred type of data collection?**

A. Continuous measurements

B. Momentary time sampling

C. Partial interval

D. Whole interval

**9. When one behavior ends, Sara starts a stopwatch and stops when the other behavior starts. This is called _____?**

A. Efficiency

B. Latency

C. IRT

D. Duration

**10. In ABA, frequency and rate are almost equal. But there is a difference. Which of the following is true?**

A. Rate is less precise than frequency.

B. Rate is more trustworthy than frequency.

C. Rate is just frequency with a time component added.

D. Event recording is the only rate.

**11. A BCBA instructs her client to purchase a glue stick, a Pen, and a Storybook from the Bookshop. When he returns, she examines his shopping bag to ensure he has bought everything on the list. The BCBA is using _____.**

A. ABC recording.

B. Momentary time sampling.

C. Whole interval recording.

D. Permanent product recording.

**12. As an RBT, you must use _____ graph for data plotting.**

A. Scatter plot

B. Line graph

C. Pie chart

D. Bar graph or histogram.

**13. Which of the following behavior is defined as observable and measurable?**

A. your client is frustrated

B. your client hits his younger sister

C. your client is happy

D. your client is an autistic child, and his aggression is because of this

**14. Your BCBA asked you to do a functional assessment using indirect measures.**

A. Conducting interviews and surveys, compiling rating scales and questionnaires

B. Observing a subject and taking data about preferences

C. Functional manipulation in an analog setting

D. All the above

**15. Following is the function of behavior**

A. Laying on the floor

B. Crying, yelling and throwing objects

C. Sensory, attention, and escape

D. None of above

**16. Your BCBA wants to adjust how the parent reacts to certain behaviors of their child. The BCBA is adjusting what.**

A. Consequences

B. Functions

C. Behavior

D. Stimuli

**17. As an RBT, you are preparing yourself for data collection; you will go for all of these except?**

A. Understanding the target behavior

B. Reviewing history from the previous sessions

C. Adjusting the behavior plan based on parent feedback before the session

D. Gathering necessary stimuli before the session starts

**18. You are an RBT who has just completed a forced choice preference assessment and successfully identified several stimuli. What must you do now under the supervision of your BCBA?**

A. You must continuously observe the behavior

B. Set intervals and measure them correctly

C. Conduct multiple stimuli preferred assessment

D. Conduct a reinforcement assessment

**19. Your client just learned the alphabet and counting. He can differentiate between both. Now he is mixing up the alphabet with counting. As an RBT, what do you think the issue is?**

A. Stimulus generalization

B. Response generalization

C. Overgeneralization

D. Response maintenance

**20. As an RBT, U conducted a reinforcer assessment under the supervision of a BCBA and determined that candy is a reinforcer for your client, but appreciation does not. What procedure would you use for reinforcers that tend to fade edible reinforcers for appreciation?**

A. Give her candy when she engages in the correct response.

B. Give her only appreciation after the correct response

C. Give her appreciation half the time and candy the other half for correct responses

D. Give her both appreciation and candy for correct responses

**21. As an RBT, you are teaching your client how to boil an egg. The steps are to fill up the pot with water. Put the. Pot on the stove, turn on the stove, wait for the water to boil, put the egg in the water, and wait for the. 7 or 8 minutes when it's done. Suppose you help your client with each step. And then reinforces your client for draining the egg. You are most likely using which intervention?**

A. Total task chaining

B. Behavior chain interruption strategy

C. Backward chaining

D. Forward chaining

22. This summer, the client you work with is on vacation. Your BCBA wants to create a schedule that aligns with his academic calendar. Each session with your customer lasts for 30 minutes. The assignment will be finished during the 30-minute breaks, and your client will get a break for the remaining time. During the 30 minutes, your customer often takes a break every 14 minutes. Which of the following reinforcements fits this treatment strategy the best?

A. FR14

B. VR14

C. FI14

D. VI 14


23. Noah's teacher once shouted at him in class when he tried to talk to his friend during a lecture. Now he is quiet when his teacher is in the class but will talk when his teacher is outside of the classroom. Is his teacher is a_____?

A. Reinforcer

B. Punisher

C. Stimulus

D. Prompt


24. As an RBT, you asked your client to fold their clothes. After 2- minutes, your client starts folding the clothes. He folds five T-shirts which takes him 4 minutes, and then takes a 1-minute break. He then folds the remaining clothes. What is the inter-response time?

A. 2 minutes

B. 4 minutes

C. 1 minutes

D. 3 minutes


25. Tokens are considered as_____.

A. Primary reinforcers

B. Conditioned reinforcers

C. Unconditioned reinforcers

D. Punishers

**26. You are driving, and you see an advertisement for Donuts. You start to crave Donuts. You pull up to the restaurant and see a sign lit up that says hot and fresh Donuts available. What is the SD in this situation?**

A. Driving down the road

B. The Billboard advertising donuts

C. Hot and fresh Donuts available.

D. You are craving Donuts

**27. As an RBT, you teach your client to greet people with "Hey". Now your client greets people with "Hello", "What's up," and "How's it going"? What is your client doing?**

A. Response generalization

B. Stimulus generalization

C. Maintenance

D. All the above

**28. As an RBT, you ask your client to throw away his trash after he finishes his lunch, and the client swipes the trash to the floor. You pick up the trash and throw it away. In the future, the client will swipe his trash. This is called_____.**

A. Positive reinforcement

B. Negative reinforcement

C. Positive punishment

D. Negative punishment

**29. Sarah will begin to cry every seven minutes. Sarah's mother consoles her when she begins to cry. For the following two weeks, you are required by your BCBA to provide Sarah reinforcement every five minutes. What kind of reinforcement is this?**

A. Positive reinforcement

B. Contingent reinforcement,

C. Negative reinforcement

D. Non-contingent reinforcement

**30. Your hands are always full when you take anything out of the refrigerator to prepare dinner, making it difficult to close the door. Depending on the situation, you may bump it, close it with your elbow, or kick it close with your foot. What describes this situation the best?**

A. Response generalization

B. Stimulus generalization

C. Backward chaining

D. Forward chaining

**31. Your BCBA asked you to work with your clients for 3 minutes before giving them a break as reinforcement. You then work with your clients for 5 minutes on a communication target before a break. Finally, you work with your clients for 4 minutes before a break. What reinforcement schedule best represents what you are doing?**

A. FI3

B. FI5

C. VI4

D. VI3

**32. You enjoy drinking a cup of tea before bed every night. To making tea, you go to the kitchen. You take out a kettle. Remove the top, then pour water on it. Afterward, place it on the stove. The stove is turned on. The water is ready when the kettle beeps after five to six minutes, and you pour the water over the tea. What does the beep stand for?**

A. The MO for pouring the water over the tea

B. The SD for pouring the water over the tea.

C. The antecedent to drinking tea

D. The consequence of grabbing the kettle

**33. The schedule in which the BCB reinforces every correct response of the target behavior is called.**

A. Intermittent reinforcement

B. Continuous reinforcement

C. Positive reinforcement

D. Negative reinforcement

**34. Your hands burn when you touch a hot bowl of soup. You won't likely touch a hot bowl of soup in the future. It's called_____.**

A. Negative punishment

B. Positive punishment.

C. Fixed ratio

D. Fixed interval

**35. As an RBT, you start your teaching interaction with your client by providing a prompt that you are sure will help the client make the correct response. Then you fade the prompts out.**

A. LTM prompt fading

B. MTL prompt fading

C. Time delay prompt fading

D. Generalization

**36. Your client learns to identify their siblings' emotions, and then they start to identify their friends' emotions. This is called**

A. Response generalization

B. Stimulus generalization

C. Maintenance

D. All the above

**37. Your BCBA tells you that response prompts may be_____.**

A. Verbal

B. Modeling

C. Physical guidance

D. All the above

**38. Your BCBA asked you to teach your client new skills. The schedule of reinforcement will be_____.**

A. FR1

B. VI2

C. FI5

D. VR1

**39.** You are teaching a client an appropriate way to gain someone's attention by tapping on the person's shoulder. Your client now taps on people's shoulders to gain their attention but often taps too hard. You start reinforcing your client for tapping softer and softer until you reach the desired tapping intensity. You are doing_____.

A. Mending

B. Imitating

C. Fading

D. Shaping

**40.** You have a client, bob. He screams when his parents try to take away his iPad. He stops screaming when his parents give him the iPad back and say, OK, one more minute. His parents want this behavior to stop. So, an extension procedure is implemented. However, Parents reported that the screaming has gotten louder and for a longer duration. What is the most likely explanation?

A. The client is experiencing an extinction burst

B. The client is resisting punishment

C. The client is resisting extinction

D. Extinction is not working

**41.** As an RBT, you are teaching a child to follow instructions and put the rapper into the dustbin. The instruction may be given right away, and then a full physical prompt may be given to the learner in order to assist them in receiving the correct response.

A. Partial physical prompt

B. Full physical prompt

C. Verbal prompt

D. Visual prompt

**42.** When RBT implements BCBA-designed programming, their top concern is _____.

A. Accomplishing the stakeholder goals

B. Following the treatment plan as designed

C. Protecting themselves

D. Protecting the client

**43. As an RBT, your prompt a client by pointing toward the correct answer. This is called_____.**

A. Gestural prompt

B. Visual prompt

C. Physical prompt

D. Positional prompt

**44. The ideal fading order is following.**

A. CRF-FR-VR

B. VR-FR-CRF

C. CRF-VR-FR

D. FR-CRF-VR

**45. Calvin does not like the sound of the vacuum cleaner and will hit his head when it is on. His mom turns on the vacuum cleaner, and only when he is not hitting his head his mom turns the vacuum cleaner off and give him his favorite candy. This is an example of_____.**

A. DRO

B. DRI

C. DRA

D. DRL

**46. As an RBT, you notice that your client is eating too much salty food while watching television while having a break. Since you are working on Minding with your client, you move the water bottle from its normal spot, and your goal is to have your client in Mind. For the water bottle, what type of teaching are you implementing?**

A. DTT

B. Incidental

C. Direct instruction

D. Tact training

**47. As an RBT, you are working with a client on the learning process. You allow your client to use his favorite character for counting. You are using_____.**

A. Demand fading

B. Behavior Momentum

C. Choice

D. Task modification

**48.** As an RBT, you teach your client to sing a song; when she is frustrated and wants a break, the student simply must sing a break instead of yelling. This is an example of_____.

A. DRI

B. DRA

C. DRP

D. DRO

**49.** The first stage is to determine the steps that are necessary to finish a task by either performing the task on your own, viewing a Board-Certified Behavior Analyst (BCBA) complete the task, or witnessing another competent individual working on the assignment. This is called _____.

A. Chaining analysis

B. Prioritization

C. Task analysis

D. Skills acquisition planning

**50.** Every time Mike goes with her mom to the supermarket for shopping. He cries for a candy bar. His mom does not give him the candy bar in the supermarket. This is called.

A. Positive reinforcement

B. Negative reinforcement

C. Tangible extinction

D. Escape extinction

**51.** Greg decided he would not eat fast food during the weekdays. The only time he allows himself to eat is Friday night and Saturday. Greg's urges to eat on Friday, and Saturday is now even greater than before. This is most likely due to_____.

A. Satiation

B. Discriminative stimuli

C. Extinction

D. Deprivation

**52. Your BCBA gives the task of hypnotizing the function of a particular behavior. The behavior is screaming. The behavior occurs when the screen is taken away from the client, when the client is given a task demand, and often when the client is by themselves with preferred items. The screaming continues even if someone checks on the client. What is the best hypothesis regarding the function of this behavior?**

A. Automatic

B. Attention

C. Tangible

D. Escape

**53. As an RBT, you are sitting in front of your client. In one hand, you are holding a doll. On the other hand, you are holding a mobile phone. You tell your client to pick one. What type of preference assessment is this?**

A. Naturalistic

B. Multiple stimuli without replacement

C. Multiple stimuli with replacement

D. Force choice

**54. For a month, you and your client have been collaborating on color schemes. Your client has now mastered the colors "red" and "blue." You are to run "red" and "blue" targets once a week rather than each session, as directed by your BCBA. What is the BCBA attempting to evaluate?**

A. Generalization

B. Stimulus control

C. Maintenance

D. Preference assessment

**55. You let your BCBA know that your client has started to avoid the job demands. Your BCBA will interview you in order to operationally describe the escape behavior. Which of the following would have the greatest operational value as an answer?**

A. When I give my client a demand, they try and get out of the demand

B. During group DTT, I place a demand on my client, and they escape the demand for two to five minutes

C. One presented with a demand ring group DTT; the client will slide out of their chair. Crawl under the table and lie down on their back

D. When presented with a demand, the client becomes upset, gets out of the chair, and goes under the table.

**56. New reinforcement and a new skill acquisition target are included in a new treatment plan that your BCBA recently introduced. If you do not understand all the plans, you should contact your BCBA. When should you get in touch with him?**

A. The next time you receive supervision

B. The next time you see them in the office or the clinic

C. Immediately, even during the session

D. Try and work out it yourself first and then reach out

**57. As an RBT, you are assisting your BCBA in conducting a target behavior assessment. Which of the following procedure would you not use?**

A. Event Recording

B. Interview

C. Narrative recording

D. Direct observation

**58. All RBTs are expected to act professionally and abstain from dual partnerships. Additionally, RBTs should foster an environment that supports efficient services. Examples of this include greeting your client's parents when you arrive, making small talk with parents, and treating the client's family members with courtesy and respect. These are some instances.**

A. Building report

B. Client intervention

C. Parent training

D. Conflicts of interest

**59. Which of the following response options should you notify your BCBA about if it happens?**

A. Your client changes or starts a new medicine

B. Your client's parents have started to argue during sessions

C. Your client has started to wake up at 4:00 AM every day

D. All the above

**60. As an RBT, you should maintain the dignity of your client. Which of the following presents maintaining client dignity the best?**

A. 13-year-old client is an excellent reader, but his program involves reading books for five- and six-year-olds.

B. In response to your client throwing their lunch on the ground. You tell them they don't get to eat anything for the rest of the day.

C. Your BCBA is discussing your client's treatment plan. Since your client is in the room, you BCB asked the client his opinion on the schedule.

D. You are toilet training at your clinic which is filled with other RBTs and clients. You leave the door wide open during toilet training because it is more convenient for you.

**61. When taking on new clients, it is best to avoid having concurrent ties and conflicts of interest. Which of the following best describes a circumstance in which you were unable to play the function of RBT in the client's case?**

A. The client is your best friend's nephew

B. The client is the brother of a client you are currently working with

C. The client is the son of the manager of the gym where you work out

D. The client goes to the same school as your daughter

**62. Your client is debating whether to send their child back to school this year as soon as classes resume. They inquire about what you believe they ought to do from your most recent session. What's the best way to respond?**

A. Refer your client to your supervisor.

B. Give the client your honest opinion

C. Tell your client you are uncomfortable giving your opinion on the question

D. Ignore the client's question and change the topic

**63. To influence behavior modification, RBTs need to be able to control antecedents. This can be done, for example, by adjusting motivational operations. Which of the following response options has nothing to do with encouraging activities?**

A. Satiation

B. Deprivation

C. Increase further behavior

D. Alter the value of the reinforce

**64. Of the following, which is the best professional language for an RBT?**

A. William was bad today

B. Will did not like the reward

C. William engaged in 3 tantrums

D. All the above

**65. It is critical to maintaining a respectful and communicative relationship with your BCBA. In which of the following scenarios would a supervisor be wrong to request an RBT?**

A. Your supervisor asks you to run by their house and pick up something they forget before you head to your session

B. Your supervisor comes down with the flu. He asks you to take over the supervisor role for the new couple of weeks while he recovers

C. Your client's mom has a question about her son's diet. Your supervisor instructs you to research diets and autism and relay that information to the client's mom

D. All the above

**66. What are the factors, other than therapy, that affect the progress of your case?**

A. Ecological variables

B. Topological variables

C. Both A and B

D. None of above

**67. For discussion on the progress of ongoing cases, _____ is very important.**

A. Incident report

B. Team meetings

C. Professional language

D. All above

**68. As an RBT, If you have a critical/clinical question regarding your case. You must ask your BCBA within_____ hours.**

A. 6 hours

B. 12 hours

C. 24 hours

D. 36 hours

**69. As an RBT, your responsibility is to always _____ the program. The program should not be created.**

A. Implemented

B. Created

C. Designed

D. Enforced

**70. Your BCBA instructs you to treat a client in the same way you would treat your_____.**

A. Teacher

B. Student

C. Friend

D. Family member

**71. The scientific approach to staff and parent training is called _____.**

A. Skills training

B. Behavioral training

C. Behavioral skills

D. Behavioral skills training

**72. _____ is a check to improve the skills of an RBT.**

A. Feedback

B. Practice

C. Reporting

D. None of above

**73. You are aiding your BCBA in modifying the treatment plan based on all the information below, apart from.**

A. Parent request

B. Records

C. Visual analysis of graph data

D. Science

**74. The first person an RBT should speak with if they are having issues with a client is.**

A. The client's parent

B. The company director

C. The supervising BCBA

D. The client's group home manager

**75. When you are explaining ABA concepts to parents and guardians, it is important that you_____.**

A. Only speak to parents when your supervisor is there.

B. Use technical language and jargon.

C. Provide weekly quizzes to parents.

D. Explain concepts using known technical language.

**76. What should you do when you are an RBT, your client or someone else is in danger?**

A. Call the client´s parents immediately

B. Implement the crisis plan immediately

C. Call your supervisor immediately

D. Implement extinction immediately

**77. The future frequency of behavior can be determined primarily by its history of consequences.**

A. Respondent behavior

B. Basic behavior

C. Operant behavior

D. Secondary behavior

**78. The best example of Respondent behavior is the following.**

A. Playing piano

B. Newborn´s pupil constriction

C. Both of above

D. None of above

**79. David is on a road trip and is counting the cows he sees. He didn't see another cow for 15 minutes after seeing the first. He saw his third cow after 10 minutes and his fourth cow after 5 minutes. What is David's total IRT when it comes to seeing cows?**

A. 15 minutes

B. 10 minutes

C. 5 minutes

D. 30 minutes

**80. Session notes are an essential component of service delivery. All the following should be included in proper session notes, Except_____.**

A. What you observe during the session

B. What you measured during the session

C. Your subjective opinion of the session

D. Anything that was mastered.

**81. SAFMEDS is being used by Rachel to prepare for the RBT exam. Her goal is to correctly guess ten slash cards per minute. Her data for today showed she completed 4-minute, 6-minute, 8-minute, and 2-minute workouts. How often do Rachel's flashcards get it right on average?**

A. 4 minutes

B. 6 minutes

C. 5 minutes

D. 3 minutes

**82. There are four fundamental schedules for reinforcing. FR, FI, VR, VI. What does the V in VR and VI stand for?**

A. The reinforcement schedule changes day to day

B. The reinforcement schedule changes at random

C. Reinforcement is delivered on an average

D. Reinforcement varies from client to client

**83. With your client, you are developing their levels of receptivity. You say, "Touch the bird," as you're seated at the table. Once the client has responded, you give feedback before saying, "touch the bird." You then repeat this three times. This is an illustration of.**

A. Incidental teaching

B. Distractor trials

C. Mass trial DTT

D. Mix trial DTT

## 84. Which is not suitable for an unconditioned punisher?

A. Biting into food that is too hot

B. Walking outside in cold weather

C. Reprimanding a student for taking in class.

D. Receiving a shock from an electric outlet.

## 85. After standing in a Starbucks line. I would like a tall, black coffee, Julia replies as she approaches the counter. This is what's known as an over-verbal operant.

A. Intraverbal

B. Mand

C. Tact

D. Echoic.

# Answer Key

| | | |
|---|---|---|
| 1.  B | 20. D | 39. D |
| 2.  A | 21. A | 40. A |
| 3.  A | 22. D | 41. B |
| 4.  B | 23. C | 42. D |
| 5.  B | 24. C | 43. A |
| 6.  C | 25. C | 44. A |
| 7.  C | 26. C | 45. A |
| 8.  B | 27. B | 46. B |
| 9.  C | 28. B | 47. D |
| 10. C | 29. D | 48. B |
| 11. D | 30. A | 49. C |
| 12. B | 31. C | 50. C |
| 13. B | 32. B | 51. D |
| 14. A | 33. B | 52. A |
| 15. C | 34. B | 53. D |
| 16. A | 35. B | 54. C |
| 17. C | 36. B | 55. C |
| 18. D | 37. D | 56. C |
| 19. C | 38. A | 57. B |

| 58. A | 68. C | 78. B |
| 59. D | 69. A | 79. D |
| 60. C | 70. D | 80. C |
| 61. A | 71. D | 81. C |
| 62. A | 72. A | 82. C |
| 63. C | 73. A | 83. C |
| 64. C | 74. C | 84. C |
| 65. D | 75. B | 85. B |
| 66. A | 76. B | |
| 67. B | 77. C | |

# Practice Test 4

**1. Kai earns a token for every two correct responses. What schedule of reinforcement is this?**

A. Continuous

B. Fixed-Ratio

C. Fixed-Interval

D. Variable-Interval

**2. Danny is working with Jake on identifying animals. Danny teaches this by sitting at a table and showing Jake 3 different pictures. Two of the photographs are not animals, while one is an animal. Danny provides the SD, "Show me the animal." If Jake identifies the correct picture, he will receive a token on his board. If he does not respond, then Danny will provide a prompt. Which teaching procedure is Danny using?**

A. Natural Environment Teaching

B. Discrete Trial Training

C. Prompt Fading

D. Chaining procedure

**3. Stevie loves animals, so his mom took him to the zoo for the day. Stevie was excited to go to the zoo! While at the zoo, Stevie was smiling and laughing while watching the animals. Throughout the day, Stevie's mom pointed to random animals and asked, "What animal is that?" What teaching procedure is Stevie's mom using?**

A. Discrete trial training

B. Stimulus control transfer

C. Prompt fading

D. Natural Environment Teaching

**4. Billy and his RBT are playing with toy cars. The RBT has a red car and a blue car in her hand. When Billy says, "I want a car, please," the RBT asks, "Which color?" What type of teaching procedure is this an example of?**

A. Discrete trial training

B. Chaining procedure

C. Incidental Teaching

D. Mand training

**5. This procedure breaks a skill down into smaller, more manageable steps.**

A. Discrete trial training

B. Task Analysis

C. Natural Environment Teaching

D. Shaping

**6. _____ occurs when some behaviors are reinforced, while others are not reinforced.**

A. Discrimination Training

B. Prompting

C. Discrete Trial Training

D. Shaping

**7. Tom is teaching Archie to identify a dog. Tom provides reinforcement when Archie points to a picture of a dog and says, "dog." Tom does not reinforce when Archie points to a picture of a cat and says, "dog." What is this an example of?**

A. Discrete Trial Training

B. Discrimination Training

C. Stimulus control

D. Natural environment teaching

**8. Prompt delays, prompting fading, and stimulus fading are all examples of...**

A. Generalization

B. Maintenance

C. Stimulus control transfer procedures

D. Prompt hierarchy

**9.** Mia would like to increase Charlie's independence by tying his shoes. Typically, she will provide hand-over-hand assistance immediately after giving the vocal SD, "Tie shoes." However, today, she waits 10 seconds before assisting. What method is Mia using?

A. Prompt fading

B. Stimulus fading

C. Prompt delay

D. Shaping

**10.** While teaching her client to wash his hands, Sarah initially uses full physical prompts, then decreases the assistance she provides until her client finishes washing his hands independently. This is an example of a?

A. Prompt fading

B. Stimulus fading

C. Task analysis

D. Discrimination Training

**11.** _____ is referred to as being able to keep a skill over time

A. Maintenance

B. Generalization

C. Stimulus control

D. Discrimination

**12.** Everly's dad is bald, wears glasses, and has a short beard. Not only does she say "Daddy" when she sees her dad, but she also calls every other bald man who wears glasses and has a short beard "Daddy." What is this an example of?

A. Overgeneralization

B. Response generalization

C. Stimulus control

D. Discrimination Deficits

**13.** Anthony has difficulty remembering what he needs to do in the morning before school, so his dad lists all the things Anthony needs to complete (e.g., eat breakfast, brush his teeth, get dressed, pack a bag, etc.). Dad hangs the list on the wall for Anthony to reference. This list is another example of.

A. Task Analysis

B. Maintenance

C. Generalization

D. Discrete Trial Training

**14. Shaping is referred to as** _____.

A. Reinforcing successful approximations of the behavior until the desired behavior is reached

B. Maintaining a skill over time

C. Emitting a response under various stimuli

D. Transfer control of behavior under one stimulus to the control of another

**15. Discrete Trial Training (DTT) occurs in a _____ environment and is _____.**

A. Highly Structured, therapist-led

B. Loosely Structured, therapist-led

C. Highly structured, client led

D. Loosely structured, client led

**16. The following are examples of behaviors that can be shaped, EXCEPT...**

A. Riding a bicycle

B. Walking

C. Talking

D. All are considered examples of behavior that can be shaped.

**17. Mikey has difficulty attending to DTT instructions at the table during ABA therapy sessions. He often will get up from the table, move around in his seat, and whine when the tasks are too challenging. Currently, the only reinforcement system in place is random breaks that Mikey can earn at the discretion of the RBT. Which of the following is the best strategy the RBT can implement to increase the likelihood of Mikey attending during sessions?**

A. The RBT can implement a token economy.

B. The RBT should block any attempts to get up from the table

C. The RBT should reduce the duration of the break every time Mikey gets up from his seat or moves around in his chair

D. All of the options

**18. Which is not considered a component of the behavior reduction plan?**

A. Target behavior

B. Replacement behavior

C. Crisis protocol

D. Client diagnosis

19. _____ are appropriate skills that are taught to individuals that serve the same function as the problem behavior.

A. Replacement behaviors

B. Maintenance goals

C. Function behaviors

D. Target behaviors

20. Every time Lily cries, her mom hugs her. When mom gives a hug, the crying increases. Now, every time Lily wants a hug from mom, she calls. What may be the function of the crying behavior?

A. Sensory

B. Escape

C. Attention

D. Tangible

21. _____ is a function of behavior maintained by access to preferred items, toys, activities or food.

A. Sensory

B. Escape

C. Attention

D. Tangible

22. _____ are environmental variables that alter the effectiveness of a stimuli serving as a reinforcer.

A. Motivating operations

B. Antecedent manipulations

C. Preferred stimuli

D. Natural factors

23. Ross is having difficulty focusing on tasks at the table, so for every other token he earns, the RBT gives Ross a mini M&M. This strategy effectively increases Ross's focus until after lunch when Ross no longer wants the M&Ms. What should the RBT do?

A. Switch up the reinforcer

B. Only give an M&M for the last token Ross earns

C. Stop giving M&Ms

D. Continue providing M&Ms for every other token

**24. The teacher wants to reduce the number of times his students get out of their seats, so he praises them when they sit in their seats. This is an example of...**

A. DRO

B. DRA

C. DRI

D. DRH

**25. Gestural, physical, vocal, and visual are all types of...**

A. Prompts

B. Stimuli

C. Techniques

D. Shaping procedures

**26. Jordan will curse at his teacher when he does not want to do his work. The following are strategies the teacher can use to reduce the behavior EXCEPT...**

A. Teach Jordan to ask for a break

B. Implement a token system to reinforce when Jordan complies with work

C. Place Jordan in time-out every time he curses

D. Ignore the cursing

**27. Every time Ava cries, her dad gives her his iPad. When dad realized that the iPad might be reinforcing Ava's crying, he decided to make a change. He now no longer gives her the iPad when she cries and, instead, ignores the behavior. This is an example of...**

A. Extinction

B. Negative Reinforcement

C. Negative Punishment

D. Positive Reinforcement

**28. Which of the following is not an example of extinction?**

A. Whenever Jeffrey engages in attention-seeking tantrums, his mom gives him a disapproving look.

B. Liz places an armed guard on Mattie's arm to prevent injury from self-stimulating scratching behavior.

C. Dad ignores his son's attention-seeking crying behavior

D. Every Tuesday, you watch your favorite reality tv show. However, the cable went out today, and now you can't watch your show.

**29.** Your 17-year-old client, Devon, does not engage in aggressive behaviors during the session but has engaged in aggression toward his parents in the past. There have been concerns about Devon's mental health; he was previously hospitalized. However, this was over three years ago, and he has since remained stable. During today's session, Devon's mood was flat, and he seemed disengaged. His appearance is disheveled, his hair is unkempt, and he has a pungent body odor. He confides in you that he has homicidal thoughts toward his parents and plans to act on those thoughts the next day. Based on this information, you feel Devon is an immediate threat to others and himself. What is the best way to respond to this scenario?

A. Call 911 or local authorities immediately.

B. Contact your BCBA immediately.

C. Evaluate the client to determine if homicidal ideation is valid, and make a decision on how to proceed with getting your client immediate help

D. Document the incident in your note, and then inform the BCBA during supervision

**30.** Julian engages in severe self-injury in the form of punching his head. He wears a helmet to block self-injury, which occurs up to 700 times daily. Julian, however, learned to remove his helmet so he could engage in self-injury. A crisis protocol was established with instructions on responding to the behaviors. The RBT is certified in Professional Crisis Management (PCM) and utilizes physical intervention strategies when behaviors escalate. Today, Julian took off his helmet and hit his head so hard that he lost consciousness and had a seizure for 1 minute. What should the RBT do?

A. Call 911

B. Perform CPR

C. Suggest that mom bring Julian to the hospital

D. Wait until Julian regains consciousness, then continue the session.

**31.** Jake, an RBT, noticed that the BCBA added a program goal to teach the client how to use the bathroom. However, the client is fully potty trained. What should Jake do?

A. Inform the BCBA

B. Make the change to the program

C. Do not collect data on that goal

D. Run the program as designed

**32. How often should the RBT communicate with their supervising BCBA?**

A. On an ongoing basis

B. Only during supervision

C. Once a month

D. Once a week

**33.** RBT Izzy is having difficulty implementing skill acquisition programs, as her client has been engaging in a high frequency of tantrums and self-injury during sessions. Izzy should...

A. Communicate concerns with supervising BCBA

B. Continue to implement the skill acquisition programs as best as possible

C. Implement a punishment procedure for tantrums and self-injury

D. Make changes to the skill acquisition programs so that they are easier to implement during times of high-intensity behaviors

**34.** The supervising BCBA implemented a new reinforcement procedure for a client. After three weeks of implementing the new procedure, the RBT on the case does not feel it is effective and has seen no change in behaviors from the client. What should the RBT do?

A. Address these concerns with the BCBA

B. Change the procedure

C. Continue implementing the procedure as designed

D. Advise the parent that the procedures are not effective

**35.** Ivan earns a point every day when he eats his vegetables. When he reaches 5 points, his parents will treat him to ice cream and a movie. The facts are an example of?

A. Token economy

B. Reward system

C. DRO

D. Shaping

**36.** A client's parents informed the RBT that they have recently separated and that one of the parents will be moving out of the house. The RBT should...

A. Add a note to the client's program.

B. Provide counsel on how to assist their child during this difficult time

C. Ask the parents why they are separating

D. Inform the BCBA

**37.** During the session, your client's parent informed you that the client started a new medication that may suppress their appetite. What should you do?

A. Stop running mealtime goals.

B. Add a program to work on increasing food intake

C. Tell the supervising BCBA

D. Collect baseline data on any time the client refuses to eat food

**38. What type of information should be included in your session notes?**

A. Behaviors that occurred during the session written in observable and measurable terms

B. The type of goals worked on during the session

C. Who was present during the session

D. All should be included

**39. Hilary engaged in tantrum behavior during the session. Which of the following is an appropriate way to describe the behavior in a session note?**

A. Hilary engages in a 10-minute tantrum in the form of crying and screaming. The tantrum occurred when access to a doll was denied.

B. Hilary got upset because her doll was taken away. She cried for 10 minutes.

C. Hilary was very emotional during the session, as evidenced by crying.

D. Hilary got sad when she wasn't able to play with her doll. It was heartbreaking to hear her cry for 10 minutes.

**40. All data and client documents should be stored _____.**

A. In a secure location

B. In a file cabinet

C. In a folder

D. At the client's home

**41. A client recently terminated services. What should you do with the program materials and completed data sheets?**

A. Return to supervising BCBA

B. Shred them

C. Keep them for seven years

D. Let the caregivers keep the materials and documents.

**42. Connie is a licensed psychologist in her home country of Brazil but recently moved to the United States to begin a master's of ABA program. She passed the RBT exam and now works part-time at a company providing ABA therapy. During one of her first sessions, Connie notices that her client displays symptoms concurrent with ADHD. This client does not have a formal diagnosis. What should Connie do?**

A. Provide the caregiver with resources on ADHD

B. Implement interventions designed to treat ADHD

C. Offer to evaluate the client for ADHD

D. Inform the BCBA

**43.** As an RBT, Ira has extensive experience treating feeding disorders through her work with a severe behavior clinic. She decided to take her experience and open an ABA clinic. She advertises the feeding program as one of their top specialties. She does not have a BCBA working for her company, so she oversees all client programs until she can afford to hire a BCBA. What should Ira do to ensure she complies with the BACB code of ethics?

A. Ira violates the BACB Code of Ethics and should stop providing services immediately.

B. Ira should hire a BCBA to oversee the clients.

C. Ira should hire other RBTs to help her implement programs.

D. Ira should become a BCBA so she can ethically run the company.

44. During supervised sessions, RBT should always _____.

A. Respond appropriately to feedback

B. Be prepared with any questions for the BCBA

C. Improve performance according to feedback

D. All options are correct

**45.** During supervision, the BCBA observed the RBT place the client in time out after the client engaged in tantrum behavior during a non-preferred demand. The BCBA advised the RBT not to use time out and why. The BCBA also recommended reviewing the current goals and protocol for responding to tantrum behaviors during non-preferred demands. The RBT disagrees with the BCBA and feels that time out is the best approach. However, the RBT does not tell the BCBA how she feels. How should the RBT respond?

A. Improve their performance

B. Explain to the BCBA why they disagree

C. Demonstrate to the BCBA how time-out is effective

D. Complain to the BCBA about the feedback

**46.** During the session, your client's dad asks you for some feedback on how to improve the client's eating habits. This client does not have any feeding goals in his program. You should...

A. Acknowledge dad's concerns and let him know you'll speak with the BCBA

B. Give dad some feedback on how he can address feeding

C. Add a feeding goal to the client's program

D. Take baseline data on the client's eating habits

**47. The holidays are around the corner, and your client's parents want to take you to dinner as a special thank you. What should you do?**

A. Politely decline the offer.

B. Accept the offer

C. Accept contingent on being able to bring the client to work on restaurant manners. You will bill the outing as a regular ABA session.

D. Accept contingent that you pay yourself.

**48. You are an RBT assigned to work with a client in a group home. This client is a 50-year-old woman who is nonverbal and does not engage in self-injurious or aggressive behaviors. The group home recently underwent a staffing change for the nighttime shift, but you only see your client in the morning. One day, you arrive at the session and notice your client sitting in her room crying. She has a bruise under her arm and appears to have wet herself. When you ask the day staff if anything happened, they cannot answer. They show you the shift notes from the night before, which do not indicate anything out of the ordinary. However, you arrive at the session every day that week to find that your client has wet herself and is crying. One day shift staff pulls you aside and informs you that she suspects one of the new nighttime staff is abusing your client. What should you do?**

A. Report to the appropriate authorities

B. Inform the group home manager

C. Inform the BCBA

D. Speak directly with the nighttime staff member accused of abuse

**49. Candace is an 18-year-old diagnosed with an autism spectrum disorder. She receives ABA therapy to help with vocational skills. During the session, the RBT assists Candace with filling out a job application. When they get to the part that asks if the applicant has a disability, the RBT advises Candace to say "yes." However, Candace said she would instead not answer since the question was optional. How should the RBT respond?**

A. Allow Candace to skip the question.

B. Advise Candace to answer the question truthfully so that the employer can provide the appropriate support

C. Reward Candace for answering the question

D. Talk to your BCBA

**50. The RBT notices an increase in their client's screaming behavior. The screaming is so loud that it interferes with daily tasks and communication. The RBT should respond by _____.**

A. Informing the BCBA

B. Ignoring the screaming

C. Providing reinforcement when the client doesn't scream

D. Taking baseline data on the volume of screaming

**51. Suzy's first day as an RBT, and she is nervous about writing the session note. Before finalizing the note, Suzy texts a draft to the supervising BCBA for review. What, if anything, did Suzy do wrong in this scenario?**

A. Suzy violated HIPAA

B. Suzy should have emailed the draft instead

C. Suzy did not do anything wrong

D. Suzy should have ensured that she used the client's initials instead of the full name.

**52. Mandy, an RBT, arrives at her client's house for the first session. When she enters the house, she is greeted by a familiar face. The individual turns out to be the client's uncle, whom Mandy had a romantic relationship within college. The relationship was noncommittal but lasted for six months. It turns out the uncle lives with the client's family. Mandy hadn't seen the uncle in 5 years, but they both remembered each other. What should Mandy do?**

A. Mandy should talk to the BCBA and ask to be removed from the case

B. Mandy should continue the case as long as she doesn't tell the family about her history with the uncle

C. Mandy should continue the case as long as she doesn't talk to the uncle

D. Mandy should continue the case. Because she already knows the uncle, rapport-building should be easy.

**53. The RBT certification must be renewed _____.**

A. Annually

B. Every two years

C. Every three years

D. Every six months

**54.  Sophia, an RBT, is asked to collect frequency data on a client's aggressive behavior during her 2-hour session. Which of the following could Sophia use to manage the frequency data?**

A. Tally counter

B. Timer

C. Calculator

D. Stop Watch

**55.  Jean collects data on every instance her client hits his head with an open hand. What type of measurement method is Jean using?**

A. Frequency

B. Duration

C. Rate

D. Latency

**56.  After receiving his fast-food order, Jeff checks the bag to ensure all items are there. What type of measurement method is this an example of?**

A. Permanent Product Recording

B. Frequency

C. Whole Interval Recording

D. Total count data

**57.  Janelle collects data on how long it takes from when she asks her daughter to clean her room to when her daughter starts to clean her room. What measurement method is this an example of?**

A. Inter-response time

B. Latency

C. Duration

D. Whole Interval Recording

**58.** Chris engages in long durations of repetitive screaming, sometimes lasting up to 1 hour nonstop. Diane would like to implement a procedure to reinforce when Chris is not engaged in the behavior for a certain length of time, but will first need to determine an appropriate interval. She takes IRT data to measure the length of time between repetitive screaming episodes. Then, she will implement a procedure to reinforce the absence of screaming for a predetermined length of time. What reinforcement procedure does Diane use?

A. DRO

B. DRA

C. DRI

D. DRL

**59.** Ana wants to quit eating sweets, so she throws away all the candy, cookies, and ice cream in her kitchen. This is to prevent her from eating sugary treats. What is this an example of?

A. Antecedent modification

B. Negative punishment

C. DRO

D. Negative reinforcement

**60.** RBTs should receive supervision for _____% of the hours they are implementing behavior analytic services.

A. 5%

B. 10%

C. 20%

D. 15%

**61.** Nina, an RBT, works with a client in the classroom 25 hours a week. The teacher, BCBA, and Nina all have a great working relationship and are aware of Nina's role as an RBT. However, during class today, there was a substitute teacher. When another student hit Nina's client, the substitute teacher reprimanded Nina for not disciplining the student accordingly. How should Nina BEST respond?

A. Nina should explain to the substitute her role in the classroom

B. Nina should do what the substitute says

C. Nina should discuss the concern with the BCBA

D. Nina should discuss the concern with the client's teacher.

**62.** Robin's client, Ellie, engages in a high frequency of hand biting. Robin blocks the hand biting whenever it occurs. Per Ellie's behavior reduction plan, Robin is to collect frequency data for each instance of hand biting. A paper datasheet is used to track the frequency of Ellie's hand biting. However, it is sometimes challenging for Robin to collect real-time frequency data between blocking the hand biting and running skill acquisition goals. Which of the following would be the best method for Robin to easily collect frequency data on Ellie's hand-biting behavior?

A. Robin should count the number of hand-biting instances in her head and then write it down on the paper datasheet.

B. Robin should collect duration data instead due to the high frequency of the behavior.

C. Robin should try using a clicker to track the frequency of the behavior and then add that number to the paper data sheet at the end of the session.

D. Robin should only collect data if there are less than two instances of hand biting per minute. Anything higher than that, Robin should not have to worry about data collection.

**63.** All of the following are ways that the RBT can prepare the environment for data collection, EXCEPT...

A. Peter prepares a paper data sheet before the session with all the goals he plans to run that day.

B. Meg uses the first 5 minutes of the session to organize the workspace and log into the data collection portal on her phone.

C. Brian is collecting data on the frequency of self-injury and the duration of tantrums. Every session, he comes prepared with a clicker and a stopwatch.

D. Christina forgot to prepare for the session, but because she's known her client for a year, she feels she doesn't need to prepare

**64.** Your client engaged in a high frequency of aggression that lasted the entire session, and you stayed an extra hour to ensure that your client was calm. Your client's mom noticed you had a rough session, and she felt terrible. She offers to take you out to the local bar for a drink. How should you respond?

A. Politely decline the offer.

B. Accept the offer

C. Accept contingent that you pay for your drink.

D. Decline, but suggest she can buy you a bottle of wine instead to show her appreciation

**65.** Regan is collecting data on her client's tantrum behavior. At 9:02 am, her client started crying. This continued until 9:30 am when the crying stopped. Regan marked the data as 28 minutes of crying. What type of measurement procedure was Regan using?

A. Duration

B. Frequency

C. Latency

D. Rate

**66.** Which is an example of a discontinuous measurement

A. Partial Interval Recording

B. Permanent Product Recording

C. Rate

D. Duration

**67.** Josie is teaching Chris to ride a bike. Josie prepares a data sheet to track when Chris rides his bike independently. The total observation time is 30 minutes. On her data sheet, Josie splits the 30 minutes into six intervals (5 minutes each). If Chris rides his bike for the entire interval, Josie places an X for that interval. If Chris rides his bike during some part of the interval but not the entire interval, then Josie leaves that interval blank. What type of measurement procedure is Josie using?

A. Partial Interval Recording

B. Whole Interval Recording

C. Momentary Time Sampling

D. Rate

**68.** An RBT observes their client's repetitive vocal behavior for a total observation period of 60 minutes. The time is split into six intervals of 10 minutes each. If the repetitive vocal behavior occurred at any point during each interval, then the RBT will place an X for that interval. If the repetitive verbal behavior did not occur during the interval, then the RBT will leave that interval blank. What type of measurement procedure is the RBT using?

A. Partial Interval Recording

B. Whole Interval Recording

C. Momentary Time Sampling

D. Rate

**69. This measurement procedure measures a behavior's effects on its environment after it occurs. It does not require direct observation of the behavior.**

A. Frequency

B. Rate

C. Permanent Product Recording

D. Momentary Time Sampling

**70. What does the horizontal x-axis on a line graph represent?**

A. Passage of time

B. Frequency of behavior occurrences

C. Location of behavior

D. Individuals collecting the data

**71. Which of the following is NOT an example of a behavior definition?**

A. A tantrum is defined as whining, screaming, and crying

B. Aggression is defined as any instance of hitting another individual with an open or closed fist

C. Repetitive motor behavior is defined as any instance of wiggling fingers and waving hands out of the context of the ongoing situation (e.g., when they are not waving)

D. Screaming is defined as any time Molly gets upset

**72. This preference assessment is when the assessor presents two items in each trial. After the individual briefly engages in their chosen item, the items are swapped out and replaced with another two items. This continues until all items used in this assessment have been presented together at least once.**

A. Multiple-stimulus with replacement

B. Multiple-stimulus without replacement

C. Paired Choice

D. Free Operant

**73. Shaping is referred to as _____.**

A. Reinforcing successful approximations of the behavior until the desired behavior is reached

B. Maintaining a skill over time

C. Emitting a response under various stimuli

D. Transfer control of behavior under one stimulus to the control of another

**74. Which of the following is an example of an intermittent schedule of reinforcement?**

A. FR1

B. VR4

C. NCR

D. CR

**75. The following are examples of behaviors that can be shaped, EXCEPT...**

A. Riding a bicycle

B. Walking

C. Talking

D. All are considered examples of behavior that can be shaped.

**76. A standardized test can be used to:**

A. Provide information on the client's behaviors

B. Provides a standard score on how client behaviors compare to those of other individuals of the same age

C. Does not provide information on client behaviors

D. It is the only assessment that can be used to determine the eligibility of services because it allows for normative data

**77. On which operant should you work first?**

A. Mand

B. Tact

C. Interval

D. Echoic

**78. The antecedent for a mand is:**

A. Generalized conditioned reinforcer

B. MO

C. Non-verbal stimulus

D. Non-verbal conditioned reinforcer

**79. In this functional analysis condition, target behaviors are expected to occur at low levels.**

A. Contingent attention

B. Contingent escape

C. Play

D. Alone

**80. Of the following scenarios, which one does not exemplify a socially significant behavior change?**

A. Tommy, five years old, elopes from his house frequently without supervision. His family lives by a lake, and he cannot swim.

B. Judy, 18 years old, has one best friend. Her parents want her to make more friends, but Judy expressed that she is content with the one friend she has.

C. Lily smokes a pack of cigarettes a day. Lily didn't want to quit until her doctors diagnosed her with COPD.

D. George doesn't know how to drive but wants a job. He wants to know how to ride a bike to get to and from work.

**81. This type of preference assessment must be run several times to determine the hierarchy of the reinforcers.**

A. MSWO

B. MSW

C. Paired

D. Forced Choice

**82. What is the difference between a direct assessment and a descriptive assessment?**

A. A direct assessment is a checklist - a descriptive is a written assessment.

B. A direct assessment can only be conducted with the client – a descriptive assessment can be conducted with the client or caregiver.

C. A direct assessment and a descriptive assessment are the same thing

D. A descriptive assessment is not a valid term

**83. The most widely used reinforcement in ABA is:**

A. Positive punishment

B. Positive reinforcement

C. Negative punishment

D. Negative reinforcement

**84.** An RBT must be supervised at list _____ of the monthly hours spent providing behavior-analytic services.

A. 10%

B. 5%

C. 20%

D. 15%

**85.** Riley works with Agnes, a 4-year-old girl with ASD. For every correct response, Agnes is given one token. When she has 5 tokens, is has earned jumping on the trampoline. What schedule of reinforcement is used?

A. FR5

B. VR5

C. CR

D. NCR

# Answer Key

| | | | | | |
|---|---|---|---|---|---|
| 1. | B | 19. | A | 37. | C |
| 2. | B | 20. | C | 38. | D |
| 3. | D | 21. | D | 39. | A |
| 4. | C | 22. | A | 40. | A |
| 5. | B | 23. | A | 41. | C |
| 6. | A | 24. | C | 42. | D |
| 7. | B | 25. | A | 43. | B |
| 8. | C | 26. | C | 44. | D |
| 9. | A | 27. | A | 45. | B |
| 10. | A | 28. | A | 46. | A |
| 11. | A | 29. | A | 47. | A |
| 12. | A | 30. | A | 48. | A |
| 13. | A | 31. | A | 49. | A |
| 14. | A | 32. | A | 50. | A |
| 15. | A | 33. | A | 51. | A |
| 16. | D | 34. | A | 52. | A |
| 17. | A | 35. | A | 53. | A |
| 18. | D | 36. | D | 54. | A |

| 55. A | 66. A | 77. A |
| 56. A | 67. B | 78. B |
| 57. B | 68. A | 79. C |
| 58. A | 69. C | 80. B |
| 59. A | 70. A | 81. A |
| 60. A | 71. D | 82. C |
| 61. A | 72. C | 83. B |
| 62. C | 73. A | 84. B |
| 63. D | 74. B | 85. C |
| 64. A | 75. D | |
| 65. A | 76. B | |

# Conclusion

As you conclude this RBT Exam Study Guide, you've delved into critical aspects of behavior analysis, learning essential concepts and strategies crucial for success in the Registered Behavior Technician (RBT) exam. This recap aims to reinforce your knowledge and provide guidance for your exam journey, while also shedding light on avenues for continuous learning and career advancement in behavior analysis.

## Recap of Essential Points Covered in the Study Guide

This study guide has provided in-depth insights into various facets of behavior analysis and applied behavior analysis (ABA), including:

- **Foundational Principles**: Understanding the fundamental principles of behavior analysis, the history and development of ABA, and the ethical considerations within the field.
- **Roles and Responsibilities**: Outlining the scope of practice, code of ethics, and professional conduct expected of an RBT.
- **Behavior Assessment and Intervention**: Exploring the intricacies of behavior assessment methods, behavior reduction strategies, skill acquisition, and instructional procedures.
- **Measurement and Data Collection**: Learning about different data collection methods, implementation procedures, and the significance of graphing and visual representation of data.
- **Exam Preparation Strategies**: Equipping yourself with effective test-taking strategies and tips for managing exam anxiety to perform your best on the RBT exam.

The inclusion of practice tests within this study guide offers you the opportunity to apply your knowledge, simulate the exam environment, and further strengthen your confidence and readiness.

### Encouragement and Tips for Success in the RBT Exam

Approaching the RBT exam can be a challenging yet rewarding endeavor. Remember, success is not only about mastering content but also about adopting effective exam strategies and managing stress.

- Stay consistent in your study routine and focus on understanding the core concepts of behavior analysis.
- Prioritize practice exams and sample questions to familiarize yourself with the exam format and types of questions.
- Employ active learning methods, break down complex topics, and allocate more time to challenging areas.
- Practice relaxation techniques to manage exam anxiety and maintain a healthy lifestyle during your preparation.

Believe in your preparation and capabilities. Your dedication and effort will yield results. Keep a positive mindset, visualize success, and trust in your knowledge and skills.

## Continuing Education and Career Growth in Behavior Analysis

Passing the RBT exam is an important milestone in your career journey within behavior analysis. Beyond the exam, continuous learning and professional development are vital in this field.

Consider pursuing advanced certifications, such as Board Certified Assistant Behavior Analyst (BCaBA) or Board Certified Behavior Analyst (BCBA), to expand your career opportunities and responsibilities. These certifications enable you to work more independently and design behavior intervention plans.

Engage in ongoing education by attending workshops, conferences, or pursuing higher education in behavior analysis. Stay updated with the latest research and advancements in the field, enhancing your knowledge and practice.

Networking within the behavior analysis community can be invaluable. Collaborate with colleagues, seek mentorship, and participate in professional organizations to exchange ideas and stay connected with industry trends and best practices.

Remember, a career in behavior analysis offers diverse opportunities across various settings, including schools, clinics, hospitals, and community-based organizations. Your dedication to improving the lives of individuals through behavior analysis is a noble pursuit, and your continued growth will contribute to the field's advancement.

As you embark on your journey toward becoming an RBT, embrace the knowledge gained from this study guide and apply it not only to excel in the exam but also to make a meaningful impact in the lives of those you will serve. Your dedication to learning, professional growth, and commitment to ethical practices will shape your success as an RBT and contribute to the positive evolution of behavior analysis.

Best wishes on your RBT exam and in your promising career in behavior analysis!

Made in United States
Orlando, FL
06 December 2024

55092896R00067